Press On

A Disciple's Guide to Spiritual Growth

Cecil Murphey

SERVANT BOOKS
Ann Arbor, Michigan

Published by Servant Books, P.O. Box 8617, Ann Arbor, Michigan 48107
Book design by John B. Leidy

Printed in the United States of America
ISBN 0-89283-129-4

In appreciation for Dixie, Kiki,
and Betty, but especially Dolly

Contents

ONE

The Call to Self-Discipline

I LEANED AGAINST the window ledge of the hospital room as Ann talked about her upcoming surgery. A lengthy telephone call interrupted our conversation.

So as not to appear to be listening, I picked up Ann's Bible, which lay on the windowsill. She had opened to Ephesians, and I read silently through two chapters. For some reason, I particularly found myself reading 4:14 again and again: "So that we may no longer be children, tossed to and fro and carried about with every wind of doctrine. . . ."

I paused and, still hearing Ann's voice trying to end the phone call, turned and stared out the window.

Two floors below, a young boy got out of a car. He had been eating a sandwich. After a few steps, he took the aluminum foil from the sandwich, wadded it into a ball, tossed it on the ground, and walked on. Seconds later, a gust of wind picked up the aluminum foil ball, raised it into the air a few inches, and carried it along the sidewalk. Fascinated, I watched. For perhaps the next three minutes that helpless foil bobbled around, moving in one direction, then stopping until a fresh breeze swept it in another direction. Eventually, it was out of sight.

Watching that aluminum foil, I thought of the words I had just read, "tossed to and fro and carried about with every wind." It occurred to me that this is the way many people live. They let life carry them along. Whichever wind blows hardest determines their decisions. When the wind lets go, they drop and nothing happens until another strong influence picks them up again. I have observed this in the Christian fellowship hundreds of times over the years. I can think of many examples.

Andy easily gets excited about renewal and commitment. He immerses himself in any programs or plans that promise help in spiritual growth. For six weeks you can count on Andy for anything—day or night. But after two months he has lost interest. Occasionally he will respond, "I don't feel led."

Rick has committed himself to reading the Bible completely through, praying every day for ten minutes, and losing forty pounds—all in the current year. But, then, Rick has made those commitments before. And failed. He means it when he says it. Yet somehow other things—sports activities, home pressures, and job demands, for example—always seem to take up his time. Consequently, he has never fulfilled any of the commitments he makes to himself. He also carries a lot of guilt inside and sees himself as a spiritual failure.

Diana has joined and left at least five churches in the half-dozen years I have known her. "I'm always looking for the Spirit at work," she said once. "I must go where the people are on fire for Jesus Christ." She is much like the ball of tinfoil, bouncing from one fellowship to another, never settled, never giving of herself, never opening herself to deepening experiences.

Others, not as flighty, easily moved, or undisciplined as Andy, Rick, and Diana, have trouble in other ways. They live by letting life happen to them. These sincere folks participate in congregations, often involved in major activities. But they yield to pressure. The pressure can be as simple as the pastor or an elder urging them to teach or to sing in the choir. Someone else begs them to attend a sharing group in a home. Another wants their help to resettle a refugee family. All fine pursuits. To which ones do they say yes? Which ones should they decline?

One such person said to me, "I'm so busy doing Christian work, I don't have time to *be* a Christian." People find themselves yielding to pressure and lacking a will of their own for two reasons. Either they do not know how to take charge of their lives, or they are afraid to. The result remains the same: external powers determine their movements.

As you read this, perhaps that is how you see yourself, caught up, tossed to and fro, and unhappy about it. You want to move forward in your Christian experience, and yet . . .

I recently talked with a small group who cried out for "something more" in life. They expressed vague dissatisfactions, but could not quite put their finger on the trouble-spot. They sensed only that they were living in a lower spiritual realm than God wanted them to. Furthermore, they had no idea what to do about it—what *could* they do? Most people experiencing this hunger have usually already gone to a dozen seminars and workshops on strengthening their Christian experience. They have participated in home Bible studies or Sunday school classes with great curriculum titles such as "Growing in Christ" and "Spiritual Development." But, though they put in a lot of activity, they seem to get nowhere.

I can't supply all the answers (I don't even know all of them for myself!), but I have learned a few things about discipline. That word, *discipline,* is the key to spiritual growth. Discipline! That sounds like some ancient monastic code or grade-school rules. I use *discipline* in the sense of learning to be, or being, a disciple. If we are going to walk forward with Jesus Christ we have to face the matter of disciplining our lives.

Certainly the Spirit intervenes in our lives—touching us, filling us, reviving us, and enlightening us—yet those experiences become only momentary events unless we learn to maintain and grow through them. We need to make those divine interventions part of an ongoing process.

Self-discipline comes easier for some than for others. No one knows exactly why. Home training undoubtedly affects us. Our culture, and even our educational background, shapes us as well. But, whether you are by nature disciplined or not, I can offer you hope. You can change. You can be a more faithful disciple. It will not be easy if you are the tossed-to-and-fro type, but it won't be impossible either!

Don't sit back and sigh: "I'm not the studious type." "I ought to do more Bible study, praying, (add whatever else you like)." "I'm just not self-disciplined, that's all."

Jesus Christ calls us to be his own. We find constant commands toward greater commitment, service, love, prayer, exercise of faith. Because God calls us, he also enables us.

When it comes to self-discipline, to a large degree it can be *learned.* We can teach ourselves. With the Holy Spirit's help we can stop making excuses and become the kind of disciples of whom he is not ashamed.

As you concentrate on self-discipline, you will fail at times. We all do. Here is lesson number one: *forgive yourself.* That is one of the harder lessons to learn. Back in the days when I first moved into the realm of self-discipline, I failed almost as often as I succeeded. Then I would mentally berate myself, "Murphey, you fouled up again!" I would heap tons of guilt on my own head.

Then, while reading the wonderful little classic, *The Practice of the Presence of God,* I found an answer that I remind myself of from time to time:

> That when he failed in his duty, he only confessed his fault, saying to God, *I shall never do otherwise if You leave me to myself; it is You who must hinder my falling, and mend what is amiss.* That after this he gave himself no further uneasiness about it.[1]

"That's it!" my heart yelled. "Outside of the Lord's help, I will fail time after time. But, with his help . . ."

I want to tell you a little about myself. For me, self-discipline has come easy. When I reflect on my childhood this surprises me. I am the fifth of seven children, and my parents presented no model of self-discipline. I can only say that somehow, perhaps in reaction to the anything-goes-whenever-it-happens attitude in our home, I developed an ability to discipline myself.

Actually, I never thought of myself as disciplined until my

seminary days. While going full time to seminary, and subsequently graduating second in my class, I also completed a master's degree in education at a local university and preached every Sunday.

At the time, it did not seem unusual to me. But as people asked, "How do you fit all those hours in?" I realized that I am by nature a disciplined person. I knew that I could always find time to do what I considered important.

It was after my conversion at age twenty-one that I began to realize that my life no longer belonged to me. Because I was God's, I had to learn to submit myself to his scrutiny. One of the first bits of advice I received from Christians put me on the right path. "Read your Bible and pray every day." They did not tell me how to do these things or how much time to devote. Later, I learned that some of them were only repeating pat phrases because they knew it was the right thing to say. Yet I obeyed their advice and set aside time every day. It meant getting up earlier each morning (I started with a safe ten minutes). Once I had established the habit, I increased my time to read and pray more by arising earlier.

Within six months after my conversion, I met Shirley, one of those Christians who cannot remember when they did not love Jesus Christ. She was faithful in her devotional life. In our months of dating, no matter how late we stayed out, when Shirley got home she took time for prayer and Bible study, even when it meant missing sleep. Her example inspired me to discipline myself more firmly.

The first few years caused me no serious problems. I knew so little about the faith that I felt I had to move quickly to catch up with those who had been Christians for years. But after nearly ten years, the Bible began losing its excitement for me. I had read it through several times and knew as much about it as any of my friends. Prayer became routine, often even dull. That is when the struggle over discipline really came into my life. I reached the place where I had to choose: drift or swim. I saw many drifters, but few who struggled against the currents. I knew a few who went through periods of intense study and prayer, and it would show in their spiritual growth. Then they would stop swimming and drift.

Someone has said, "First you shape a habit and then a habit shapes you." I continued to pray and read. Sometimes I felt bored and wondered if I was really getting anything out of it, but I kept going. Then, what I can only call a "season of refreshing from the presence of the Lord" (Acts 3:19) occurred, and I realized that my struggle had been worth it.

Now, years later, I acknowledge that some days my Bible study still seems empty, pointless, and mechanical. My prayers take on a routine sound that makes me wonder if I am boring God too. But I also know that such attitudes are part of the growing process. I have kept on (not always perfectly, but I *have* kept on). I have yet a great distance to cover before I reach that place of discipleship that Jesus spoke of in Matthew 5:48: "You therefore must be perfect, as your Heavenly Father is perfect." But after a quarter-century of struggling along, I have learned a few lessons about discipline, and these are some of the basic ones:

1. We all have differing capacities. Obvious? Of course, but I did not grasp that for years.

For instance, a year after my conversion I read about "Praying Hyde," an early missionary to India. His biography said that John Hyde spent four or five hours daily on his knees, and remarkable answers to his prayers followed. The book implied that if I wanted to follow Jesus Christ totally, I would learn to pray at least three hours each day. I reasoned, "If Hyde could do it, why can't I? He was only a man, too."

I determined that I would pray every morning for at least three hours before getting involved in my day's activities. I arose by 4:00 A.M. and prayed until nearly 7:30. For eight mornings I kept my vigil. The flush of victory, however, was the prelude to failure. Most mornings I started out fine but soon fell into a gentle sleep, awakening only because I had cut off the circulation in my legs. Furious with myself and filled with remorse, I heard my inner voice remind me, "You failed again."

One morning, I awakened after sleeping almost the entire time. I begged the Lord's forgiveness. I felt like Peter, James, and John must have felt after sleeping in the garden during the time of Jesus' great agony. There must be a secret, I kept thinking, a system or a gimmick I could use to keep awake.

Then one morning a conversation went on inside my head:

"You're not Praying Hyde, you know."

Of course I'm not, but . . .

"You're Cec Murphey."

I know that.

"Then stop trying to be someone else."

Of course! Such an obvious answer. I would never be like Praying Hyde. Why should I imitate him? I had neither the natural bent nor the temperament for the more contemplative life. I am more of an activist. Some types spend much of their time praying for things to happen. Others, like myself, go out to make them happen. And we are both acceptable to God.

2. We all have different needs. Once I acknowledged I was not Praying John Hyde, I had to find my particular level. I returned to ten minutes of prayer and at least that long in daily Bible study. As I sensed my need for more private time with the Lord, I added minutes to my devotional time.

One morning I had read my Bible twenty minutes and felt satisfied. Then I thought, "But surely this isn't long enough." I had hardly finished saying those words aloud when it occurred to me, "Who says so? Do longer periods of time hold special blessings from God?"

Perhaps I can get more out of a book in twenty minutes than my wife can in thirty. She is slower and more analytical. Does that make me better? Her more spiritual? It means only that we are not the same. I may not need as much time as my wife. We both pursue God at our own pace. We have both committed ourselves to *daily* fellowship with God. From that point, it becomes a matter of our individual need.

3. We all have different levels of commitment. My level of commitment to Jesus Christ helps determine the amount of time and the quality of that time spent with him. As I sense my level of commitment deepening, I become aware of a greater need for fellowship with the Lord.

No two people feel or act alike. I don't believe in trying to set up a standard by which to judge a person's spiritual level. That is where the Holy Spirit deals with each of us on a personal and intimate basis. I never even like to tell anyone how much time I spend or how I divide that time. It may lay on some a burden heavier than they are able to carry. It might discourage others who think every committed Christian spends more time every day in prayer and study.

I don't plan to give you a list of rules in this book. I will, however, suggest ways to increase your commitment by your own acts of self-discipline.

I purposely use the term *self*-discipline. God has given us intelligent minds. While the Holy Spirit can and does intervene in life, I am convinced God seldom does for us what we can do for ourselves.

God doesn't cram his word into our hearts. The psalmist says, "*I* have laid up thy word in my heart, that I might not sin against thee" (Ps 119:11). We do what we can with what we have, then God takes over. Or, to paraphrase Paul, someone plants the seed in our hearts, we nourish it, but God gives the increase (cf. 1 Cor 3:6).

This is a call to discipleship through self-discipline. Yet as I write about self-discipline I do not advocate a life of stringent living, with hundreds of daily demands laid upon us. The self-discipline I advocate follows the call of Jesus, who said that if anyone wished to follow him, "Let him deny himself and take up his cross daily" (Lk 9:23). For me, the practical outworking of that call comes through disciplining myself.

The process of self-discipline showed in our first family bouts with handling finances. Shirley and I were both working, yet by the time we paid off our bills we always seemed to have nothing left. For the next six months we recorded every cent we spent. I discovered that I wasted a lot of money on small things, especially dime or quarter items. As we monitored our spending, we saw several areas of waste. We corrected them by setting up a budget. Today we no longer follow a rigid budget. We don't need to. We have been handling our finances long enough that we are aware of how we spend our money. We have learned to discipline ourselves in the way we spend, save, and give.

Self-discipline may have a negative sound to it. It often does at first. Yet it involves three positive and significant steps. First, we see where we fail and analyze why. Second, we resolve to deal with the problem with a plan of action, so that with God's help we make a change. Third, we form new patterns. This style points us to a fuller relationship with Jesus Christ.

TWO

The Spirit's Role

"I DON'T UNDERSTAND the Holy Spirit," Katie said. "You mention him a lot in your preaching, but it's all just words to me."

This young Christian, eager to follow Christ, was beginning to ask the right questions. For many, talking about the Holy Spirit means repeating creeds or singing hymns, but with no practical significance. "Just what kind of difference is the Holy Spirit supposed to make in our *lives*?" she asked. Only when we ask that question, honestly seeking an answer, do we begin to touch the role of the Holy Spirit. Until then he is little more than the third member of a vague, though divine, Trinity. Our prayers and our church hymns all center on God the Father or Jesus the Son.

Who is this Holy Spirit, aside from being part of the Godhead? Jesus spoke about the Spirit, saying that after his own death and resurrection, the Spirit would come. That same Spirit would point people to Christ and teach them about the Savior. He would convict of sin and dwell within believers.

That is part of his work. What else does the Spirit do? What is his role? Similar questions were thrown at me when I stood before more than a hundred ordained ministers for examination for my own ordination. One pastor in particular kept pressing me to speak about the Holy Spirit.

I gave him the classical answers: Regarding salvation—God planned it, Jesus made it possible by his death, and the Spirit applies it to our lives. When it comes to sin—God warns against it, Jesus paid for our failures, and the Holy Spirit convicts us. I continued down the list and concluded with this: When it comes to growth—God wants it to happen, Jesus urges it, and the Spirit brings it about. I also talked about the Spirit as the one who provides the power we need for victorious living. I passed the exam, of course, because I gave the right answers.

The significance of the Holy Spirit only started to be apparent to me when I sought to grow. I thought little, if at all, about the Holy Spirit until a deep spiritual hunger overtook me. That is the only way I know how to express what happened. During a week's vacation, I shut myself away from everyone. I prayed and read constantly. For some reason I could not explain, I read several books about the Holy Spirit, a subject I had not thought much about previously.

All during that week, I cried out, "Give me more of yourself, God." I still vividly remember those days. They were a pivotal point in my spiritual pilgrimage. I felt hunger in my heart for the "something more" in my Christian experience that found no satisfaction in faithful church attendance or heavy involvement in activities. I reminded the Lord of his promise in Matthew 5:6, "Blessed are those who hunger and thirst for righteousness, for they shall be satisfied."

"Satisfy me, God," I pleaded. Within the next few weeks, events transpired that radically changed my life. The presence of Christ became so real that, for weeks at a time, I felt a spiritual presence with me. The thought from Psalm 16, that the Lord is "at my right hand," was with me more than at any other time in my life. The Lord was so real that I could not think of him as "up there somewhere." I knew that he stood next to me.

During that time, prayer not only became habitual but natural. When any question arose, I found myself repeating the promise from James 1:5, "If any man lacks wisdom, let him ask of God." I asked.

The most dramatic event was the change in my attitude toward my father. Always a self-contained person, he had never expressed affection for me or any of us children. I had grown up thinking that he hated me. He didn't hate me, though it took me years to find that out. As my attitude changed, I genuinely learned to care about my father and, eventually, I was even able to tell him that I did.

I didn't think of these events as direct answers to my retreat prayer. Only weeks later, as I thought again of that time of intense hunger for God, did I realize that many changes had begun taking place in me only days after my prayer.

The Spirit produces the growth in our lives. As we inch forward, we learn how dependent we are on him to energize and push us onward. When we seek to discipline ourselves, we learn again that we need his power in our lives. I can't explain growth, but I know that somehow the Holy Spirit brings it about.

For me, the major avenue of growth in commitment to Jesus lay in the area of spiritual self-discipline. Part of the work of self-discipline has meant a growing awareness and sensitivity to the Holy Spirit. He speaks in quiet tones. I have had to get away from distractions to hear him speak.

The Holy Spirit does involve himself in everyday activity, but not to bring us into bondage—not even the bondage of knowing his will. I know people, quite seriously, who will not get dressed until they pray about what to wear. They will not wash a dish or sweep a floor until they sense the Spirit telling them to. The Spirit does not work that way. God does not do for us what we can do for ourselves. The Spirit won't tell me when to turn off the heat while I am cooking, or to fill my tank with gas when the gauge registers empty. I can do those things for myself.

But at times, we do need specific direction beyond our common sense. And, beyond guidance, we need the Holy Spirit empowering us on a day-to-day basis, helping us to carry out our commitments.

The most dangerous trap for most of us is that we rarely think we really need the Holy Spirit in our daily lives. We may say we need him because we know we are supposed to, but on a practical level we ignore him or operate without him. For instance, I have had to wrestle with the attitude "I can do it by myself." I do not consciously exclude God. I just think I can do the task on my own without his help.

Often I can. Why should I ask God to help me read my Bible daily if forming the habit proves no problem? Or to help me faithfully pray for people and events each day when I already do. I personally do not need to plead, "God, help me to get up so I can go to church today" (though some people have to pray that way every Sunday).

I can remember a time when I had to pray for just that kind of help. I had worked nearly three years in Kenya, East Africa, with no breaks, no days off, no rest. Every day I found more things to do and more opportunities to proclaim the gospel. During those years a group of Africans and I had started at least a hundred new churches.

One morning I awakened without the strength to get out of bed. I had pushed myself so long that I had exhausted all my resources. God had not pushed me that hard. I had worn myself out by not seeking the Spirit's guidance. It not only took much prayer for the Lord to give me needed strength for that day, but I also had to learn to listen to the Spirit during the following weeks for wisdom to know when to stop working. God calls us to a full commitment. We will never find that intimate relationship without relying upon his Spirit.

Yet we all make promises to God and to ourselves which we do not have the ability to keep. When we acknowledge that we cannot keep them, despite our self-determination and self-discipline, then the Holy Spirit can and will empower us. It is at that place of *recognized* need that the Holy Spirit does his work. He is the energizer, the motivator, the power-giver. *And he is available.*

As we become concerned about spiritual self-discipline, we also become more conscious of our need for the Spirit's work in us. If he is truly the one who "effects sanctification," as my seminary professor often said, then we need a better understanding of this relationship. *Sanctification* means either being set apart for a holy purpose or the process of growing in holiness. As believers, the Spirit separates us from the world, making us truly the church (in Greek, *ekklesia*—"the called out"). But what does that mean in practical terms? God intends for us to be fully his, and we become more fully God's people as we live like him.

Here is how it works in a particular situation. Dave, a thirty-year-old, comes to the realization of his need for God in his life. He undergoes a "conversion experience." At first a Sunday-morning-only attender, Dave begins to sense a need for something more in his life. While that is the Spirit at work, Dave senses only a dissatisfaction about his spiritual life. In his desire to progress spiritually, he begins to pray and read the Bible regularly and involves himself in congregational activities.

After a few weeks, he neglects Bible reading one morning, promising himself that he will read twice as much the next day. At the end of three months Dave discovers that he has stopped reading the Bible on a daily basis.

If the hunger still gnaws at him, he can either ignore it or do something about it. He may start his self-discipline regime again, only to fail once more. These ups and downs may go on for years, as they do for most people until they recognize they are trying to handle spiritual battles with their own strength.

"Lord, help me," he finally prays. "I can't discipline myself. So many other things get in the way." When he genuinely calls out for the Lord's help, Dave begins to be able to discipline himself.

The Spirit does not work through magic incantations that fill us with supernatural power. Instead, he gives the wisdom and the strength to discipline ourselves. Even then, self-discipline does not come easily. We struggle against the evil powers of the world (cf. Eph 6:12). But it is always worth it. We enjoy life more. We feel better about ourselves. We have an inner peace, even in the midst of struggle, knowing that God promises special blessings to the *overcomer*. We are encouraged to persist, to keep on striving. Hebrews 12:1-3 compares the Christian life to running a race. We are exhorted to cast off anything that weighs us down. Philippians 3:13-14 tells us not to look back but to always press onward.

To move into true spiritual discipline is a cooperative effort. The Spirit provides the motivation and the wisdom. He is there to struggle with us, but we need to put on the whole armor of God (cf. Eph 6:10-20) as we battle spiritual enemies.

This truth of cooperation with the Spirit showed itself plainly during our missionary service in Kenya. Occasionally people would come to the country, expressing their eagerness to work for Jesus Christ. I would suggest enrolling in Swahili school or hiring a national to tutor them in a tribal dialect. During our six years in Africa I never knew a single person who spoke a language fluently without working at it. I could not document a single instance of the Spirit "giving" someone the language, despite the enthusiastic boasts of some who thought the Spirit would teach them without their putting any effort into the process.

How do we move beyond laziness and frequent failure? Realize that the Spirit *guides* but does not *push.* The Spirit teaches those who are obedient. We do what we can, then rely on the Spirit to do the rest: "Pray as if everything depends upon God; work as if everything depends on you."

Every once in a while I encounter preachers who tell me that they never prepare for a sermon or a lesson. Instead, they depend upon the Holy Spirit, citing Jesus' words in Luke 12:11-12. (Incidentally, in context, Jesus referred to disciples being brought to *court.* He told them not to worry about what to say in *defending* themselves.) Often, though they preach for long periods of time, even hours, their content could be condensed into ten minutes.

When I went through that phase, teaching or preaching without preparation, I rambled too. Nowadays, I carefully write down what I am going to say (even though I do not read my manuscript). I go through the sheer discipline of preparing exactly what I want presented. When the actual speaking comes, I try to keep open to the Spirit's intervention. When I have done everything I know to do, I *can* turn it over to the Spirit.

Will Dave ever become a disciplined Christian? *Only if he chooses to.* If he cares enough to guard his time, channel his energy, offer himself to the Spirit, then things can happen. First he has to work. He must offer what he has, like the boy with the meager lunch who opened his provisions to Jesus. Then God will multiply his abilities and use them as he desires.

If any Christian wants to live the self-disciplined life, it involves making choices. It means giving up things in our lives—even good things.

In my own case, a dozen years ago, while a full-time pastor and enrolled at a university preparing for my Ph.D., I felt God wanted me to write. I could not write for publication, complete my academic work, and faithfully minister to the flock. I left the university.

We often have to say no to legitimate and enjoyable activities. One friend gave up golf. "I can get the relaxation in an hour's racquetball," he said. "It was a matter of how God wanted me to use my time."

We will find ourselves making such choices frequently, not between good and bad as much as between good and best. As we make the choices, we sharpen our focus. We seldom become experts in ten fields, but we can live more closely to God.

For me, that's the most important thing anyway!

THREE

Teach Me, Lord

AT LEAST TWO TIMES in their lives, most Christians cry out, "Lord, teach me to pray." On those two occasions they behave very much like the first disciples. The Twelve, after following Jesus and seeing his power at work, sensed a lack in their own lives when they discovered Jesus in prayer (cf. Lk 11:1). "Lord, teach us also," they cried.

Most of us first cry out for teaching at the point when we begin our pilgrimage toward Jesus Christ. As we enter into a personalized relationship with him, we find our tongues thick and our minds confused. We simply do not know how to talk to him.

I recall my own experience. Away from home and in the military service, I didn't know any Christians to ask for help. Even if I had, I would have been too embarrassed to ask anyway. For months I slipped into a darkened chapel every night. Invariably I would start with words such as, "God, I don't know how to pray, but . . ." I thought I needed a formula or an instruction manual. I felt uncomfortable and unsure of how to proceed. Yet an inner hunger would not let me back away without making contact with the divine.

Prayer, I would learn later, is like acquiring any new skill. We start awkwardly, quite unsure of ourselves, and move self-consciously. Yet as we progress, assurance grows and self-consciousness disappears. During the early days of my Christian experience, I met a couple with a two-year-old son. The child, just learning to speak, used mostly nouns and verbs, but enough so that he was understood. As the child used his language, he improved in his facility. Through being around others and conversing with them he was able, by the time he was four, to speak in complete sentences with clear enunciation. I suddenly knew that that is the way prayer works. I felt somewhat comforted, realizing I would learn to pray with greater facility.

If we grow in our experience with Christ, we do learn to pray. There are many aids in the learning process.

The most obvious help, of course, is that when we attend a church or any religious function, we hear others pray. Their expressions, their attitudes, their formality (or lack of it) teach us. By their example, they also show how significant prayer really is for them.

Shortly after my own conversion, I attended a church where, at midweek services, the same four or five would pray out loud, often for as long as twenty minutes each, in Elizabethan English. The rest of us knelt, eyes closed, trying to concentrate (or even just to stay awake). Later, I visited another church for an evening service. Several people prayed, but in contemporary language without seventeenth-century tongue twisters such as know*est* or want*eth*. I sensed that those people had a warm relationship with Jesus Christ and talked to him as if he stood next to them.

I learned about prayer in other ways. About that time I bought a book on prayer and hunted in bookstores and the public library for others on the topic. Someone gave me a list of all the prayers in the Bible, and I carefully read the entire context. Reading how Abraham, David, the Christians in Jerusalem, and Paul talked to God stimulated me toward more serious prayer. Others have found help through seminars, cassettes, groups designed especially to pray, asking questions of more advanced believers, reading the autobiographies of Christian leaders.

But the best way to learn about prayer comes through actual praying. We can read about how to drive a car and have people tell us what it feels like to zoom down the highway. But it means nothing until we actually get behind the steering column, insert the key, and turn on the engine.

I practiced praying—practiced in the sense of doing it every day. Not only in set times of prayer such as worship services and my own devotional time, but throughout the day my mind turned to God. I learned much about prayer in those days. I also realized that I would never fully exhaust everything God can teach me. For months after my conversion, I continued to pray, "Lord, teach me. I have so much to learn."

In the beginning, I put the emphasis on *quantity* prayer. If I prayed hard enough and often enough, surely God would hear and answer. The pastor of the church we attended stressed the importance of praying constantly. He frequently challenged the congregation to set aside a weekend for prayer and fasting, with a coordinated schedule, so that someone was always praying. "If we get enough people praying for revival," he said, "it will come." While I did not know much about the Bible, I questioned his theology. Only weeks before, I had read Jesus' rebuke to the Pharisees: "They think that they will be heard for their many words" (Mt 6:7). God doesn't pay attention to the volume of prayer. Peter's first letter, quoting freely from Psalm 34, tells us that God's eyes are upon the righteous and his ears open to their prayer (cf. 3:9-12). I was learning.

I discovered verses which encouraged me to pray. Jeremiah 33:3 exhorts us to call upon him and he promises to show us greater things than we have known before. Those who have clean hands and a pure heart can worship and receive blessings (Ps 24:3-5). By forgiving others, we can pray aright (see Mk 11:25). When husband-wife relationships are not right, for example, it hinders our prayer (1 Pt 3:7). I was learning.

After a time, I fit into the routine of church life. I probably prayed no less and no more than others. Along with others, I rejoiced in prayer. I felt momentary despair when I did not get responses I asked for. Then I would remind myself that no is a response. I was growing.

If we continue to learn and grow we reach a second stage in our relationship with Christ. We discover that we know as much as others about prayer. We can pray silently or in public withou nervousness. Prayer has become not only a habit but a way o life.

That is more likely to have been the situation when the twelv disciples asked Jesus to teach them to pray. Like them, when w cry *out of experience,* "Lord, teach us to pray," we are far mor serious. We don't plead because we are strangers to the habi We don't cry out because we have not frequently been involve in devotional activities. It is precisely because we *have* praye that we plead. We are on the growing edge of our lives.

We are no longer content to mumble, "Bless our family" o "Help Jane," although we can still use those words. We ar moving toward a deeper concept of prayer.

We are not even asking the same questions we asked befor The first time, we wondered if God existed. If so, did he reall answer prayer? How can I get my prayers answered? Now ou plea comes from a gnawing hunger. "God, I need more of you Teach me about yourself. Show your power at work in my life. We find ourselves yearning for a deeper relationship. Th deeper relationship does not come as we compare ourselves t others. It is a personal hunger—satisfied only by him. An often the pangs are so deep we find it difficult to tell others.

This second plea of "Lord, teach me to pray" grows out o our perceived lack of commitment. We know we have empt places in our lives which we have not yet allowed God to fill. W know by experience that we are not those who always "hunge and thirst after righteousness."

We also realize that we are not going to have mountainto experiences every time we talk to the Lord. We do not even as for a particular kind of experience. We simply want more o him. Fireworks don't go off every time I kiss my wife. Tha doesn't mean I kiss a slab of concrete. We all have our emotiona highs and lows. Sometimes we are more sensitive than others But we pray and we yearn for an ever closer walk with Christ We yearn to pray without ceasing—not as quantity prayer, bu as quality prayer. We pray as an expression of unbroke fellowship.

Our growth enables us to move through the hard places of life. We still feel the pang of disappointments but we recover more quickly. We become more sensitive to people's needs. We learn to listen to God speaking in hushed tones.

This deeper level becomes the goal of the disciplined Christian.

Jesus gave his disciples what we call the model prayer. Congregations in historic denominations pray those words every week. It is a good prayer. Yet I wonder if that is how Jesus intended it to be used. When we compare the prayer as written in Matthew 6 with Luke 11, we find it slightly different. Could it be that Jesus wanted to teach them more the *concept* of prayer than to give them a formula?[2]

I have no answer from the Bible, yet obviously the disciples *saw* something in Jesus' life that they wanted for themselves. More than mere power, could they have sensed the closeness he enjoyed with the Father? Did they suspect that he had more than an ordinary relationship with God? Was that what they wanted?

I can think of four or five people who have had that special kind of glow about them. When I heard them pray aloud, I sensed they enjoyed an intimate relationship with God, reaching beyond where most of us stop. Outwardly, their words sounded no different than others. They did not scream or whisper. Nothing I could objectively point to showed that deep contact with the Father, but some kind of indefinable witness within me knew it.

The first time it ever happened was when we stayed two nights with a pastor in northern Wisconsin. It was a terrible time for him to have us visit. We came in the middle of a severe winter storm, his wife was ill with a high fever, his older children were in school, and he stayed home to manage the house, clean, cook meals, and care for their infant son.

In the middle of the morning I opened the bathroom door and saw him on his knees, rinsing diapers in the toilet bowl, quietly thanking God for his love. Very quietly, I backed out, thankful he had not heard me. I felt as if I had intruded on holy ground.

Seeing him in trying situations, I sensed a deep tranquility about him I had never felt in another person before. He played no games to deny frustration. He accepted his situation and thanked God; the adverse circumstances made no obvious difference to him.

What I sensed in that man makes me wonder if the disciples had a similar (though probably greater) experience in their travels with Jesus Christ. They lived with a man of prayer and knew it, and wanted that prayer life for themselves.

We will not all be people who pray for long hours at a stretch, nor do I think we have to be. Some people make contact with God in seconds, while others need a gradual warm-up period. But if we are determined to be disciplined and in contact with God, prayer has to be a top priority. No one becomes a disciplined pray-er by accident or natural talent. It is a habit to cultivate and work at.

If you are not regularly (*daily*) spending time in fellowship with Jesus, I want to offer a few helps on getting started.

1. Start small, form the habit. You can always add more time.

2. Commit yourself to pray every day. Tell two or three friends. Ask them to pray for you to be faithful in this commitment.

One friend, concerned because of his lack of discipline, made a contract with me. Every morning for one week, I called him at a pre-arranged time to make certain he was awake. The next week he called me. "I'm awake," he said, and hung up almost immediately. After a month, he said, "I don't need to do this any longer. I've formed the habit."

3. Are you an owly bird or an early bird? If you are a wide-awake-in-the-morning type, plan your prayer time shortly after awakening. If you need a lengthy period to shut your mind off before you sleep, set your time at night. Or find some convenient time in the middle of the day. But make it a same-time-same-place habit, especially in getting started. You can modify later on.

4. *Make a prayer list.* Keep it short by writing down four or five names. Each day pray specifically for each name. Don't settle for "bless" and "guide" prayers. Think of a definite need in each of those lives: Bill needs a job; Elaine wants help in staying on her diet to lose eighty pounds. Needs change, but make your requests as specific as possible.

Don't forget to put your own name on that list. After all, you are an important person—one of those souls for whom Jesus Christ died.

5. *As a variation, pray for yourself as a third person.* My friend Woody taught me this. "I used to feel so selfish praying for my needs all the time," he said. "Then one day it came to me. If I were someone else, I wouldn't hesitate to pray for me."

One morning I prayed for myself this way: "Lord, Cec has to make a decision about ———. Help him hear only your voice as he decides what to do."

6. *Remind yourself: prayer is more than asking and receiving.* It is that certainly—we ask and God answers. But it is also fellowship with Jesus Christ. Prayer provides an opportunity for us to search our hearts and know more about ourselves. When we see the weeds sown in our heart, we can call upon the Good Gardener to ruthlessly destroy them.

7. *Ask God to teach you.* Tell him of your desire for fellowship with him. Ask him to increase your hunger.

8. *If you have trouble staying awake, walk while you pray.* Pace the room or walk outdoors.

9. *Determine that nothing will hinder your growth in prayer consciousness.* Reinforce that by asking God to help you to be faithful: "Lord, teach me to discipline myself *for you.*"

While I was working on this chapter, two men in our congregation started a whispering campaign against me. I tried to confront them but they denied any ill feeling or evil intention toward me.

As I jogged, I was memorizing 1 Thessalonians 5:18 in Greek. (English: "In everything give thanks, for this is the will of God in Christ Jesus for you.") The message got through to me: "Lord, I give thanks to you even though I don't understand what's happening. I'm going to learn from this experience and become stronger in my faith and in my commitment."

Over a period of several weeks, the whispering died out, one man left the church and the other recently invited us to dinner! I never had to defend myself.

10. Forgive your failures. God does. Often we are harder on ourselves than God is.

I try to pray faithfully and daily. Occasionally an unexpected disruption occurs that prevents my time of fellowship with the Lord. I have learned to say, "Lord, I missed being alone with you this morning and I'm sorry. Tomorrow I'll do better." I make no promises I cannot keep. I do not try to double my time the next day. I have simply lost a unique opportunity for fellowship with the Lord that I can never recapture.

11. Ask God to make your prayer time a period of fellowship and not a burden. In earlier days I often prayed out of duty. Sometimes I felt it was a drag talking to God and did it simply because all good Christians pray. In more recent years I have been enjoying being with Jesus Christ. I frequently ask him to make our time together a period of fellowship. Naturally some days turn out better than others. Now and then I simply don't feel like praying. But I know silence doesn't bother God and I sit quietly, allowing my mind to light on a topic it chooses.

I can think of times when I spent most of my prayer time singing songs of praise. Recently, while on vacation, I walked along the ocean, listening to the waves beating against the shore and feeling the salty spray against my bare legs. An old hymn, "This Is My Father's World," ran through my mind. I must have sung it half-a-dozen times.

I still have much to learn about prayer. In fact, I wonder if there is not a third time to cry out, "Teach me to pray, Lord." Perhaps when we have learned to enjoy fellowship with Jesus Christ and have a comfortable and established daily schedule, the inner being will cry out, "Lord, teach me to pray," meaning:

grant me a newer dimension; increase my understanding; deepen my fellowship.

I hope I will discover a dozen such stages in life when it is necessary to plead, "Teach me to pray, Lord."

FOUR

Hiding the Word

"I'M TIRED OF HEARING people tell me to read the Bible. I've tried it a hundred times and I can't understand it," Will said.

"I start out all right," Martha added, "but I get bogged down with a lot of things I don't understand."

I understood their dilemma. When I started my Bible reading, I had no one to help me. I was a sailor, away from home, and had picked up a New Testament in the chapel. None of my friends were Christians. On two occasions I talked to chaplains. One of them spoke so far over my head that I had no idea what he meant. The other kept saying, "You are moving in the right direction. Keep it up." But he never offered any practical help. Most of my understanding came through trial and error, through asking, browsing in bookstores and libraries. I had determined to read the Bible every day until I understood it.

Serious, ongoing Bible study is no easy task. We can easily pull out a printed list of verses to read when we are angry, lose a loved one, or feel rejected. I have seen such lists, and, for beginners, they are a good place to start. But as one friend says, "They band-aid the immediate symptom but do nothing for a long-term illness."

When our children reached elementary school age, someone gave us a box of Precious Promises. We tried the Precious Promises as a good way to start our day together. At breakfast each family member selected a verse and read it aloud. Each morning we had five wonderful promises, but reading only promises reminded me of having a meal with nothing but dessert. We need a more balanced diet for growth.

We need a systematic study that includes sections that make us aware of our sinfulness, that remind us of victory, that exhort us toward faithful service. Reading the Bible is one of the divinely chosen ways God has given for us to grow in our faith (Rom 10:17; Ps 119:105). We also learn from incidents in the past (1 Cor 10:11). Because the Bible is primarily a testimony o God's dealing with his own people and not a textbook of history science, or politics (although informative on many levels), we learn by reading how the ancients related to God. We can learn from their mistakes as well as from their victories.

For most Christians, however, the *why* question does not pose the problem. We may have other reasons for wanting to know more about the Bible. We may want to speak more knowledgeably (cf. 1 Pt 3:15). We may want to evangelize our neighborhood.

Once past the *why,* we need to ask *when?*

As in prayer, the same answer applies. If we are determined to understand the Bible, we will form the same-time-same-place habit. I know, for instance, that when I get up in the morning I will pray and read my Bible. I may have a busy day planned, but time in the Bible takes priority. For a long time I fought the pressure to jump immediately into the tasks of the day. I finally realized that I would have demanding situations every day, and that I needed the Bible to help me cope with those situations. "You can get back on schedule tomorrow" is one of the most deadly temptations. Stifle it.

When I first started to read my Bible, I used to pray "Open my eyes, that I may behold wondrous things out of thy law" (Ps 119:18). Later, as I used helps such as commentaries, I added "and close my eyes to those things which distract or lead me from thy truth."

The third question is *how*? I can offer several suggestions on how to read the Bible.

1. Get a modern translation. Some think that only the King James version is true and inspired. It's beautifully translated and no other version in the English language has its sweep of language or poetic flow. This version, translated in 1611 on the orders of King James I of England, has a noble history behind it. But a new Christian said to me recently, "When I read the King James Version it's like trying to read Shakespeare—and I never did understand anything he wrote."

Aside from the difficulty in understanding archaic word forms, there has been a change in the meaning of some words. For example, in 2 Thessalonians 2, the apostle Paul writes about the Son of Perdition being revealed in the last times. In verse 7, we read: "For the mystery of iniquity doth already work: only he who now letteth will let, until he be taken out of the way." Modern translators put it this way:

> Rebellion is at its work already, but in secret, and the one who is holding it back has first to be removed before the Rebel appears openly. (Jerusalem Bible)

> For the mystery of lawlessness is already at work; only he who now restrains it will do so until he is out of the way. (Revised Standard Version)

> The Mysterious Wickedness is already at work, but what is going to happen will not happen until the one who holds it back is taken out of the way. (Today's English Version)

Each of these versions makes it clear that "to let" meant to "hinder or restrain." Today "to let" has come to mean exactly the opposite!

Ancient Greek and Hebrew manuscripts, including the Dead Sea Scrolls, have been discovered since 1611, greatly advancing biblical scholarship. This enables us to reduce the small number of errors in textual transmission to even smaller numbers.

The New Testament was deliberately written in *koine*—a more colloquial Greek, and less grammatically pure. Being the language of the common people, everyone understood it. That is the strongest reason for using a modern translation: so that people can read and understand without having to constantly consult dictionaries, theological treatises, or the learned. Naturally, there are portions that are difficult to understand. We may need to get help. But most of the Bible, when translated into everyday language, makes itself quite clear.

2. Get a Bible handbook. The forerunner, *Halley's Bible Handbook,* has been updated countless times over the past fifty years and is available through most Christian bookstores. Henrietta C. Mears, in the early 1950s, authored *What the Bible Is All About,* subtitled, "An Easy-to-Understand Survey of the Bible." More recently, Leslie Peyton wrote *A Layman's Bible Digest.* Most religious publishers have short surveys or summaries of each book of the Bible. These one- or two-page statements give an idea of the content of each book.

In recent years, study Bibles have become popular. From my own experience, these are not nearly as helpful. Many of them use the King James Version and espouse a particular theological slant that tends toward a rigid, this-alone-is-what-it-means viewpoint. Furthermore, I have a great respect for those who lived in those centuries between the New Testament and the present. These study Bibles generally ignore what the church theologians have taught. While Christians scholars of the past were not infallible, they are worth reading!

Before purchasing any book of helps, ask around. Ask your pastor or a Christian friend. Find a Christian bookstore and browse through its selections.

3. When you start Bible study, have a plan. Choose a simple portion of the Bible first. I usually suggest reading Mark's Gospel because it is a straightforward narrative, with less theological interpretation than the other three. People frequently suggest new readers start with John's Gospel. I do not. John presents the most theological view of them all. Why not concentrate first on getting the factual data of the faith? As we know the content, we then can ask, "What does this mean for my life?"

After Mark, go on to Acts. Then try other portions of the New Testament. I always advise, "Study Revelation last. A proper understanding of the book comes only after you have *thoroughly* immersed yourself in the images and languages of the Old Testament." I also tell them that the prolific John Calvin wrote a commentary on every book of the Bible *except* Revelation. That omission ought to tell us something!

4. *Set goals for your reading.* You might decide to study a page or a chapter a day. You may want to give yourself a week or more to read Mark's Gospel. Whatever the pace, set goals. I discovered years ago that when we set realistic, attainable goals for ourselves we tend to stay with them. We also often feel a flush of inner pleasure when we know we have accomplished a task.

5. *Seek out a Bible study group.* Many churches now have such groups meeting informally in homes. Neighborhood groups study over coffee. There are offices where a weekly Bible study goes on during the lunch hour or before work starts. Perhaps you could ask an individual who has a grasp of the Bible and the ability to teach it to assist you in starting your own group. Invite friends or neighbors in.

With informal study groups, we have found in our congregation that it works best to have a starting *and finishing* date. Currently, I am teaching a six-week course on knowing God's will. When finished, we will break up the group, have a short rest, then announce a new study. This gives some people the opportunity to drop out and new ones to come in. It also eliminates the burden of "Oh, it's Tuesday again."

6. *Memorize.* One aspect of Bible study that seems neglected today, yet that holds much meaning for me, is *memorization.*

Simple Bible study books provided a great foundation for me. A local church pastor helped me. So did Christian friends. But I'll always be most thankful for Barry's encouragement. Barry, the son of a pastor, had strayed from his childhood teaching, then experienced an exciting conversion while serving in the Orient. When he transferred to the naval station where I was, we enjoyed a close fellowship together. Since Barry had a good foundation from his childhood, he introduced me to a particular Bible memorization program.

"Thy Word have I hid in mine heart, that I might not sin against thee" (Ps 119:11), incidentally, was the first verse I ever memorized! When I started the program my original goal was to commit to memory one verse a week. Once I started memorizing I enjoyed it so much that I learned nearly four hundred the first year. Unfortunately, I did not keep reviewing them and cannot quote all of them today. Yet many of them remain hidden deep within my heart. And, frequently, when a question arises, I find myself quoting one of those verses I learned more than twenty years ago.

As I memorized those verses, going over them phrase by phrase, it became a form of meditation. I not only sensed that growth was taking place but that God had made himself more real to me. I typed each verse on a quarter of a 3x5 card, which I carried in my pocket. During idle moments of my day—walking down the street, sitting at a stop-light, waiting for someone, or standing in the long lines characteristic of the military—I had my Bible verses handy. "On his law he meditates day and night" the psalmist says of the person blessed by God (cf. Ps 1:1-2).

When I started jogging, I discovered that my mind concentrated on my legs, the distance yet to run, the time, and the amount of miles covered. The more I thought of those things, the more tired I became. Now I do almost all of my memorizing on the hoof. And it has done wonders for my jogging! I can now put in up to ten miles while I learn new verses or review old ones.

When it comes to memorization, I find most people resistant. Their resistance is partially due to their dislike of the learn-by-rote method of their childhood educators, who forced them to memorize poetry, dates, and lists. Even today, thirty years after high school, I can still recite the first lines to Chaucer's *Canterbury Tales* in middle English. Educators have used this method for centuries. It probably accounts for the uncanny bility of the ancients to memorize and repeat tales, legends, nd facts, word for word, through dozens of generations.

For all the good reasons to memorize, people still offer xcuses.

"Memory work is too hard."

"I don't have time."

"I never could memorize well."

"Memorizing is boring."

Despite all the excuses, I am convinced it is the best way to ide God's word in our hearts where it can grow and enable us ɔ become more Christlike.

For most people, memorizing *is* hard work. But it is true that e become what we think. Whatever we fill our minds with is hat comes out of our mouths and motivates our actions. Every me we go over the same scriptural phrases again and again, we re giving God an opportunity to speak to us through those ords.

An example may help. On a long drive, I decided to emorize 1 John 4:20. As the words "he who does not love his rother" went through my mind, the Holy Spirit convicted me. brother's name popped into my head, and I could not erase it. He's obnoxious," I said, and tried to go on with my emorizing, but I knew God would not let me escape. Anger nd resentment had built up for several months and lay tucked eep inside. I gave up, stopped at the next phone booth, and ade a long distance call.

For me, memorizing scripture has proven to be one of the ost rewarding forms of getting into the Bible. Here are some ings I have found helpful in committing the words of cripture into my heart.

a. Write them out. (Or better, type them.)

b. Start with a limited goal. Plan to memorize four or five erses, ten at most. Don't think about whole chapters. Establishing the habit is more important than getting results.

c. As you memorize, it gets easier. The hardest verses to learn re the first ones. Each time you successfully memorize an ntire verse and can repeat it (along with the reference!) letter-perfect, you make it easier to learn the next verse.

d. Remind yourself often: "I'm forming a good habit. I'
hiding God's message in my heart."

e. Allow yourself no excuses. You can't memorize? Nonsens
Do you know the names of your coworkers? What about th
lyrics of your favorite hymn? Do you know your own addres
and telephone number? You had to memorize them!

f. Review. That is the secret of memorizing. Review ever
day. The sooner you review memorized material, the easier it
to retain it.

I used to carry a card of just the references. Every time
learned a new verse, I wrote down the reference. Each day I di
a warm-up exercise by reviewing between ten and twent
verses. After a few weeks I had to go back and relearn a few
them. So what? It's all the Bible!

g. Say your verses out loud as you memorize. I discovered th
vocalizing (even by mumbling or sub-vocalizing) aided m
tremendously. We remember not only what we *think* and *sa*
but we also remember what we *hear.*

h. Pick easy verses first. If you do not already know th
familiar ones such as John 3:16, Philippians 4:4, Ephesian
2:8-9, start with them. Work on the harder verses as yo
progress.

i. Refuse to be discouraged. Even if it takes you a full week
memorize and retain a single verse, you have spent that time i
fellowship with Jesus Christ, in his Word. You have filled you
mind with holy thoughts. If you memorize a verse and a wee
later discover you have forgotten part of it, don't give up
Re-memorize it until that verse becomes part of you.

j. Read Philippians 4:8—then memorize it.

k. Devise tricks for yourself to facilitate memorizing. In grad
school someone taught me to memorize the five Great Lakes b
using the key word *homes*: *H*uron, *O*ntario, *M*ichigan, *E*rie, an
*S*uperior. When I committed Philippians 4:8 to memory near
twenty years ago, I thought of a memory jogger—*the juple*
That made-up phrase, after omitting the vowels, reads: *th jpl*

"Whatsoever things are *T*rue, whatsoever things are *H*onest, whatsoever things are *J*ust, whatsoever things are *P*ure, whatsoever things are *L*ovely, whatsoever things are of good *R*eport . . . think on these things."

This is called a mnemonic device—a word, a phrase, a sound—something that aids the memory. The more off-the-wall the device, the more readily you will remember. We usually remember the unusual and ignore the things we see every day. Whenever I attempt to commit a verse to memory (and those with lists prove the most troublesome), I look for ways that will make me think of something unusual.

For instance, I had trouble with the list of nine terms in Galatians 5:22-23 (the fruit of the Spirit). After all, when you have nine different and unconnected words, it's not easy to keep them in mind—or in order. I eliminated the first three: love, joy, peace. We hear that trio all the time and in that order; it presented no difficulty. That left me with only six. *Self-control* appears last on the list. I thought, "None of the others do any good unless I end up controlling myself." That left only five words. I thought of their first letters: pkgfg. Why not "a package of fool's gold?" The phrase doesn't make sense, but it does make it easier to memorize. There I had it: love, joy, peace, followed by a package of fool's gold (patience, kindness, goodness, faithfulness, gentleness), and I ended up with self-control.

Another trick, especially for the musical, involves singing. Set the verses to music. The psalms certainly were meant to be sung. I sing several but with one unbreakable rule: I use only the biblical words, no paraphrasing and no interpreting, though I do allow repeats (to emphasize certain phrases).

My mother-in-law used to teach remedial reading. She discovered she could teach children the basics of reading by singing. From there she taught them to sing Bible verses that she set to music. My own children could sing/say dozens of verses long before they had completed their first-grade reader.

Memorize. Hide the Word of God in your heart and mind.[3]

> Blessed is the man who walks not in the counsel of the wicked, nor stands in the way of sinners, nor sits in the seat of scoffers; but his delight is in the law of the Lord, and on his law he meditates day and night. (Ps 1:1-2)

Do yourself a favor—become one of the blessed!

FIVE

Signs, Symbols, and Sacraments

SHORTLY BEFORE my twenty-second birthday I joined a Baptist church. Even though I already understood the gospel and my own relationship to Jesus Christ, I was asked to go forward, kneel, and repeat what was called the "sinner's prayer." After that, I received baptism. The final step involved giving an account of my conversion experience to the deacons of the church. Then they notified me that I had been numbered among their members.

Once a month, always the last Sunday, we celebrated the Lord's Supper. Frankly, I did not like that Sunday. For one thing, it meant that the service lasted nearly half an hour longer. I got no special meaning out of sipping juice and chewing a crumb of bread. The pastor told us every month that these two things reminded us of and represented to us the death of Jesus. Nevertheless, they meant little to me.

In that church, and in the churches among which I traveled for the next ten years, we believed in a plain style of worship. We wanted no fancy gimmicks. We wanted nothing cluttering our minds or our senses. We were so afraid of breaking the first commandment against making idols that we banned paintings of Jesus from the places of worship. Oddly enough, we allowed teaching pictures in Sunday school, showing Jesus' birth, youth, baptism, crucifixion, and ascension.

I probably would have remained in that mind-set if it had not been for a friend who invited me to his church. I went primarily to please him rather than to worship God. After all, it was an Episcopal church and, as such, it violated all the rules of simple worship. Episcopalians burn incense during the service. They have statues, candles, and stained-glass windows. Being a good Protestant, I endured the service, not hearing much of the sermon. Afterward I asked my friend, "Can't you worship God without those things?" He smiled. "That's not the question. Why not ask, 'Can I worship God *better* with them?' " At the time I shrugged, concluding that tradition and idolatrous practices had led him away from pure and direct contact with Jesus Christ himself.

I might not have thought seriously again about symbols in the church except for an incident with my wife's mother. She had become seriously ill, and it seemed that she might not recover. Fortunately, she did pull through, and a few weeks later I sat next to her bed and talked. She had placed the well-known Sallman's head of Christ across from her bed. "Mom," I blurted out, "How—how could you have that . . . ?"

"You don't know what comfort that picture gave me," she said. "I'd lie here in the stillness of the room and stare at the picture. At times I felt I could see Jesus moving out of that picture and coming toward me."

"But, that's—that's bordering on idolatry," I protested, and readied myself to fight for theological orthodoxy.

"I know only that as I looked at the picture, it comforted me. That picture brought Christ closer to me." She added, "I didn't worship the picture, but it helped me center my thoughts on the Lord."

For once I had the sense not to argue. I thought about her words. Months would pass before I began to change my thinking. Years passed before I went from toleration to appreciation. Today I no longer call such things distractions but aids—aids to a greater sense of worship. They can aid rather than hinder.

In more recent years I have become aware of the significance of symbols in our lives. All of us know the American flag. I have a three-year-old grandson who already knows that the golden arches represent the fast-food kingdom. Television and films have long told us that the roaring lion, the mountain peak encircled with stars, and the lady with the torch all represent giant film studios. All these symbols, logos, and representations make us think of a particular product, object, or person.

Symbols have invaded the evangelical world as well. Some of the most conservative Christians I know have auto tags with an image of a descending dove or a cross. One pastor who would never allow stained glass windows wears a ring with the shape of a fish, and the Greek word *ichthus,* one of the most ancient of Christian symbols. Many women, and increasingly men, wear crosses on chains around their necks. They plaster their car bumpers with religious signs and symbols. In many Protestant churches Chrismons have become increasingly common. A shorthand term for Christ monogram, these ornaments representing Jesus' life or ministry hang from Christmas trees.

In our church, a group of women makes these symbols out of styrofoam and sews on gold sequins. During the Advent season our tree displays such symbols as a descending dove, a cross, an empty tomb, and the Chi Rho (the first two Greek letters for the word Christ).

Logos. Trademarks. Signs. Symbols. Sacraments. All of these things point to something beyond themselves. They are not the reality but point us toward that reality.

Symbols tie in with what scholars refer to as the "means of grace." They all agree that this list includes baptism, communion, the Bible, and prayer. Many of them also include fellowship with others (the communion of saints). The means of grace are divinely appointed channels (means) by which we receive his blessings. That is, we grow through observing and participating in prayer, worship with others, in reading and hearing the Bible preached. When I grasped the meaning of that phrase *means of grace,* it opened up a new spiritual dimension for me.

While not trying to advocate changes in the theological stances of earlier generations, I have learned the value of other symbols in my own Christian growth. Now, as never before, I can sit quietly in a church and appreciate the beauty of stained glass. Months ago I sat in a balcony of a monastery while the monks chanted, and felt a sense of beauty through their simple worship. Tears filled my eyes.

In my own search for a fuller commitment to Jesus Christ and a desire for greater discipline for myself, I have begun to appreciate anything of a concrete nature that turns my thoughts toward him. One night our lights went out and we ate by candlelight. Throughout the meal I thought of Jesus saying, "You are the light of the world" or, "I am the light of the world." Staring at the candle became for me a means of grace.

What do these symbols, sacraments, or means of grace do? I tried to explain this recently to a friend and did not seem to get through to him, until I thought about our old garden.

My father farmed until he lost everything in the Great Depression. Moving from the Southwest to the Midwest, he worked in a factory. But until the year he died my father always planted vegetables—far more than our family could have used. We children sometimes resented having to help plant, weed, and harvest all those vegetables, but it was part of our routine of life.

In the fall, Dad plowed under all the dead plants, leaving them to rot until spring. Each year he rotated crops, adding fertilizer. Once I asked him, "Dad, why are you putting all that smelly cow manure in the ground?"

"Helps make things grow," he said and continued his work.

I thought about it for a while and, not understanding how such a thing could happen, asked, "But how do you know it helps things grow?"

Dad paused and, probably trying to figure out how to answer me in simple language, said, "I know that they don't grow well unless I use fertilizer."

That is the best explanation I can give about the means of grace. We cannot specifically point to cause-and-effect. We use these means to help us grow in our commitment to Jesus Christ.

We can only conclude that we would not grow as quickly or as strong without them.

1. That's my first reason for awareness of symbols and sacraments: *they enable us to grow.* For me, the use and value of symbols has taken on the most meaning in the sacrament of the Lord's Supper.

Christians call it by all sorts of terms—the eucharist, communion, the Lord's Table. Protestant churches generally recognize only two sacraments (communion and baptism), though Roman Catholics have seven. But whether two or seven or even fifty sacraments, the most common and widely accepted is the Lord's Supper.

Each church body has its own tradition concerning the frequency of observance. Roman Catholics and Disciples of Christ have this as an integral part of their Sunday worship. In my own denomination (Presbyterian) we have it quarterly, although some congregations choose to have it monthly.

We also observe it differently. In some liturgical churches, people come forward, kneel, and drink from a common cup. The priest places bread on their lips or in their uplifted hands as they symbolically pose in the form of a penitent. In other Christian churches, people remain in their pews while officers distribute cubed bread and serve grape juice in plastic cups. But whether wine or juice, whether round wafer, cubed white bread, unleavened crackers, or pieces from a single loaf—the symbol remains.

At the Last Supper, Jesus said, "Do this, as often as you drink it, in remembrance of me" (1 Cor 11:25). This implies that he intended the sacrament for our continued use on a regular basis. For me, this enactment of the eucharist became a matter of spiritual development. Not only have I since learned to look forward to the times when we as a congregation participate in the sacrament, but I see it as an ever stronger and more significant influence in my life.

A little background about the sacrament first.

Sacrament, from the Latin *sacramentum* and the equivalent of the New Testament word *mysterion*, means symbol. The idea of a symbol is that it represents something else, in this case a spiritual truth. The Church of England Catechism defines the word as "an outward and visible sign of an inward and spiritual grace." The Westminster Shorter Catechism reads, "A sacrament is an holy ordinance instituted by Christ; wherein, by sensible signs, Christ and the benefits of the New Covenant are represented, sealed, and applied to believers." A sacrament points beyond itself to something greater. When we observe the sacrament of the eucharist we touch and taste an outward sign which points to the work of Jesus Christ.

When we observe the sacrament, it symbolically re-enacts the death and resurrection of Jesus Christ. It recalls to us, in vivid pictorial form, his love and death. When we eat the bread and drink the wine, we are taking into ourselves the life of Jesus Christ.

Today, denominations differ greatly on the theology as well as the enactment of the supper. Roman Catholics hold to a literal change; some Baptists see it purely as a memorial; others stand between the two positions.

Without splitting theological hairs over the issue, I will simply assert that the sacrament is one appointed means by which we recognize and appropriate God's love for us. We perceive this in the amount of emphasis we put upon the sacrament.

2. Sacraments are given by God for our use. As created beings we are capable of the highest good. At the same time we are by nature disobedient people. If we were not prone to waywardness we would not have to work so hard at disciplining ourselves!

Our natural inclinations, when confronted with God's will move toward disobedience. We do not think of it that way. We are more subtle. We offer hundreds of excuses, but none of them are more than excuses. "I'll do it tomorrow. I'm too tired today. God, you understand my weakness." We progress in our spiritual maturity when we enter into a life of self-discipline. We can call it by terms such as commitment, full surrender, or sanctification, yet we progress only when we submit our wills to him.

As I become aware that God himself gave us the Bible, gave us access to himself through prayer, provided the sacraments—if I wish to grow, I need to take advantage of what he offers.

3. It is a serious error to neglect what may enhance our growth.

This winter we had a flu epidemic in our community. I don't recall ever having had flu or any kind of debilitating sickness that hit like this attack. I kept saying, "It will pass away. I'll get over it." For nearly two weeks I went to the office every morning. By noon I gave up and went home to bed—then back the next morning. It took me three weeks to recover. By contrast, my friend Betty, as soon as she began feeling the ill effects of the flu, went to her doctor. Within three days she had overcome the worst effects of the infection.

In the same way, Jesus Christ has provided for our healing (i.e., sanctification, growth). It is up to us to take advantage of the prepared medication.

It takes faith in Jesus Christ to bring us into his kingdom. It takes not only faith but commitment to enable us to enter into a fuller life with Christ. Paul writes about the mature in Christ as contrasted with the immature. He often speaks of babies and adults, full-grown sons as contrasted with children. In 1 Corinthians 3, the apostle writes about people who build their lives upon the foundation of wood, hay, and stubble: they make it into the kingdom, *barely*. By contrast, others, because of their commitment and obedience, will inherit a rich reward.

The means of Christian growth are available to us. If I genuinely see these sacraments, symbols, and means of grace as opportunities for spiritual growth, I will make use of them.

SIX

More than Food

I AM NO EXPERT on fasting.

My anxiety level forces me to make that clear before I write anything more. I have fasted on several occasions with varying success. I have also talked with people who fast regularly. Part of what I write here comes more from their experience and my theological understanding than from my own experience.

I first became conscious of fasting as a Christian discipline when I met Greg, a man with an inborn bent. He is introspective and somewhat withdrawn. I discovered almost by accident his frequent habit of fasting.

We both started college the same year. I was a veteran, married, and four years older, but we shared most of the same classes. Greg, being single and not one who made friends quickly, often visited our apartment. My wife Shirley nearly always invited him for a meal.

On one occasion Greg simply said, "No, thanks."

Greg, tall and lanky, and the possessor of a stomach that had no bottom, had surprised us.

The next day he again refused.

"Something wrong?" I asked.

"No," he said, and changed the subject.

"This isn't like you," I persisted.

For a few seconds silence filled the room until Greg answered, "I'm fasting for a few days."

"Fasting? You don't need to lose weight," I said.

"Nothing like that. I have a problem I'm struggling with. I've decided not to eat for three or four days until I discover what the Lord wants me to do about the situation."

"Oh," I said. Frankly, I thought Greg's behavior a little strange. Until that time I had never personally known any Christian who fasted for spiritual purposes. Even though I had read about fasting in the Bible, no one in the churches I had attended practiced it, or if they did, they certainly never talked about it.

During the next year I discovered that Greg fasted regularly, usually for short periods of time. He did it carefully and without ostentation. No one knew he was fasting unless we particularly asked him. He made it a secret thing between God and himself (Mt 6:16).

I began to study and read about fasting. To my surprise, I discovered few books on the subject—especially by modern writers. When I consulted literature from the early church period down through the monastic era, they frequently mentioned fasting and assumed it was part of spiritual discipline. Yet modern believers apparently ignored it.

Fasting, when done for the right reasons, becomes part of spiritual self-discipline. The very act places a hunger for God above natural, bodily needs.

I saw this throughout the Bible. Moses fasted. So did Elijah, David, Jehoshaphat, and the people of Nineveh after Jonah preached to them. Ezra insisted upon the whole nation going through a period of fasting. Moses told the people to make the Day of Atonement (Lv 23:27) an annual day of fasting and national repentance. At other times, prophets called the entire nation to a fast (cf. Joel 2:15). Paul stated that he fasted often. We have examples of fasting practiced by the early church, such as when they selected their first missionaries (cf. Acts 13:2).

Despite all these examples not a single verse ever lays upon the church a command to abstain from food. I liked that. If not commanded, it laid no burden upon me. It meant no guilt to combat if I did not fast. Yet a time came in my own life when I needed no commandment. I fasted for two days without hinking much about food or self-denial. I fasted out of a deep ense of contrition.

I had failed God by an act of disobedience which had hurt hree other people. I felt ashamed. Although I apologized and hey forgave me, I felt no better. For me, it was not just a single ıcident, but an occasion that forced me to face my frequent ailures.

To make matters worse, the four of us were traveling together or two weeks. I had to be part of the group every day. I badly vanted to return home on my own, but for practical reasons it vasn't possible.

For the next two days I hardly spoke to the others. I refused o eat, simply saying, "I'm not hungry."

In retrospect, I am sure they sensed what was going on with ne. They did not push me to eat. For two days they largely gnored me. I sat in a corner of the backseat and spent most of ny anguished time in privacy and silence. Early on the morning f the third day I awakened earlier than the others. I felt a sense f joyousness.

I'm forgiven! Those words rang through my heart again and gain. I knew the Lord had forgiven me before I began the fast. ut my inner pain, revolving around my *proneness* to disobey, ept me crying to God for help: "Why is it taking me so long to et better?"

During those two days I understood Job when he declared, I have esteemed the words of his mouth more than my ecessary food" (Job 23:12).

Another time to fast is when we feel the need for a definite nswer from God. We are troubled in soul and food has no place n our thoughts. When his illegitimate son, born to him by athsheba, was dying, David stayed in his chambers, neither ating nor bathing. He pleaded with God to spare the life of that hild. When the infant died, David got up, bathed, ate, and esumed his normal duties. God had given him an answer. But ntil that moment, he went through an intense struggle. He humbled his soul."

We sometimes fast when we need direct guidance, the special

kind of guidance that involves major decisions in life. More tha one missionary tells of yielding to the call of God only after protracted period of prayer and fasting. One couple wanted be certain they were in God's will to marry (they had a numb of obstacles that would easily have indicated they should not They agreed to fast and pray until they arrived at an answe They are happily married, more than twenty years later!

Only once do I recall that I specifically fasted for guidance. had been going through a dry spiritual wasteland. I had bee restless, feeling I should make a career move, but nothir seemed very clear. I decided to fast and spend every possib minute in prayer and in studying my Bible until God spok Fasting was not easy. Desire for food constantly nagged at m Fortunately, a phone call came in the middle of the second da giving me an answer.

Sometimes we may choose to fast as an act of spiritu discipline. One friend used to do this regularly. Every thr months he would go away for a two-day private retreat. Or time he said, "I get so filled with the world and its attitudes th every so often I need to get away and cleanse my soul." I suspe that the Pharisees fasted, at least originally, for the same reaso Their abstention showed their triumph over their own app tites. Refraining from the normal pleasures of life made the truly "the separate ones," which is what the word *Pharis* means.

Anna, who constantly prayed and fasted in the templ appears to be the kind of person who gave herself to God in th way (Lk 2:36-37). Paul also referred to his own frequent fastin (cf. 2 Cor 11:27). I have assumed that for them abstinan became as much a matter of discipline in their own life as it w for any other purpose (1 Cor 9:27).

We also fast when we are more hungry for God than f anything else. As important as food is in our life, we voluntari abstain because we crave something more than food. This a makes our priorities clear. In leaving the normal things of lif the good things, and even the necessities, we truly seek first "t kingdom of God and his righteousness" (Mt 6:33).

The first time I fasted it came about because of my deepening hunger for God. I was young in my faith and knew little about Jesus Christ. I read my Bible faithfully, memorized scriptures, and read anything of a religious nature that I could get my hands on. A few months before my discharge from the military service, I experienced such a hunger in my heart that I didn't know what to do about it. I talked to the pastor of the church where I had become a member. I had plenty of leave-time coming and wanted to spend time away from everyone where I could read and pray. He let me use an office.

For two weeks I came to that office every day. I prayed and read. During that period I ate a breakfast of toast and coffee and a light evening meal. I ate only because I felt I should, not out of any desire for food. My hunger for God was so strong that food had no appeal. By the end of the second week I sensed no dramatic response from God, nor did I expect any. I felt at peace, knowing that I had moved toward a deeper commitment to God. In retrospect, I can see that my eventual decision to enter the ministry came out of that period.

Friends, more experienced, tell me that fasting often begins with just such an undefinable spiritual hunger. As that hunger persists they set aside time to be with God and to refrain from food. One man told me that his desire to serve God and to be used by him became so strong that he went on an indefinite fast. "I became so desperate for God's power to work in my life and for his Spirit to lead me that I cried with deep anguish of soul." He kept crying out to God, "I will not stop this fast until I have peace from you and know what you want me to do." He reminded me of Jacob wrestling with the angelic being. He struggled all night and cried out, "I will not let you go until you bless me."

Sometimes our hunger for God becomes that strong. We cannot let go and the hunger persists so that nothing else is as important to us as being in harmony with Jesus Christ. We need to be careful, though, not to pray, "I'm going to fast *until* . . . ," in a spirit of blackmail. Fasting was never intended as a means of manipulating God to give us something. God doesn't *have* to do anything for us, though he may encourage us to pray with suc fervor. If so, it is for his purposes, and he gives us the stamina t continue our fast.

And when we fast it changes us. Moses came down from th mountain after six weeks of fasting. His face so glowed that the had to put a veil over his features because it hurt their eyes. W may not experience such obvious physical changes, but whe fasting is honest and sincere it does make a change in us. W have learned about life's priorities. We have demonstrated t ourselves that our commitment to God exceeds our physica need.

While fasting appears throughout both the Old and Ne Testaments and we read similar accounts in the lives of grea saints, for most people fasting is an unknown thing. Occasion ally people will ask, "How do you fast?" Numerous books hav been written in the past decade on the topic. They argu whether we should make it a complete fast (no food or water) c a partial fast (no food but water or juices to retard dehydration My purpose does not involve answering those questions. M fasting friends differ on their answers. They agree, howeve that fasting tests our commitment, strengthens our will towar self-discipline, and keeps us in the tradition of the people c God.

If, or when, you feel the need to fast, and have never done it, suggest four things to keep in mind.

1. Choose an attainable goal, such as one day. Unless you feel strong urging from God to break totally from normal routin and isolate yourself for prayer, one full day provides a sufficier challenge.

Learning to fast as spiritual self-discipline works in much th same way as learning to read the Bible or pray. We start wit small doses, always building and disciplining ourselves fc bigger challenges.

People are surprised to discover how easy fasting can be. On friend said, "I learned that food didn't have to control my life. She had been nearly fifty pounds overweight, and yielded to an temptation for food. "I'm learning to treat my body responsibly," she said. "I can resist false hunger pains and I feel closer to Jesus."

2. Don't make vows you cannot keep. Some people get so zealous to move ahead in the spiritual life that they try to start with more than they can handle. Make no vow to God for a three-day fast unless you are positive you can do it. It is better to say, "God, I'd like to fast for a day or two, and I'm depending upon you for strength." This produces a more positive effect. Then if you try to fast for two days and for some reason become too weak, nauseated, or simply discouraged, you can give yourself permission to stop. However, if you vowed to fast for three days and make it only half that time, you have to wrestle with guilt and failure.

3. Keep fasting private. Fasting is a private matter between the individual and God. When you forge ahead in your spiritual growth, the natural temptation is to tell everyone of your newfound discipline and to constantly urge, "Just try it." As I see it, the inner disciplines are not topics of frequent conversation. We should not blatantly tell everyone all our personal experiences. It may be a subtle way of pointing to ourselves and our newfound spiritual level. We shouldn't use fasting to prove something. If we are obedient and self-disciplined we won't have to tell people how often we fast, how long, or the victories we experience. They'll sense Christ's presence in us.

4. Fast as an act of self-discipline. Paul wrote that everything is lawful, though not everything is expedient (1 Cor 6:12). We have no specific command to fast. We can eat eight meals a day and, other than answering to accusations of gluttony, we will probably not have violated any spiritual laws. We fast as a way of freeing ourselves from our appetites, from the seemingly harmless pleasures of life that hinder our spiritual growth.

5. Let God teach you about yourself. You will learn how emotions determine decisions instead of calm, reasoned arguments. You will discover whether you follow God because of good feelings and rewards or out of true commitment. When you shut yourself away from others, with no caffeine to stimulate you or sugary foods to pick you up, you gain insight about yourself. You are at your most vulnerable.

For the average Westerner, fasting probably demands more self-discipline than we recognize. The media bombards us with ads, slogans, pictures, and tunes trying to lure us into the purchase of soft drinks, candy bars, cereals, and hundreds of other frozen, canned, and prepackaged foods.

One frequent food-abstainer said, "Fasting reminds us that we really don't live by bread alone, but, more importantly, that we do need the words from the mouth of God."

That word is good enough for me!

SEVEN

Money

"NOTHING TELLS ME MORE about a Christian's commitment to God than looking at the person's giving level," the chairman of our annual budget program said.

While I am not sure I can fully agree, our giving level does indicate, if not the level of our commitment, at least our self-discipline. We live in a world of pressures, lures, and subtle enticing toward spending, acquiring, and accumulating. A distinctive mark of self-discipline lies in resisting those pressures and giving faithfully to God.

There are many ways to view the matter of giving. Below are examples of three attitudes I have observed in the lives of serious Christians.

1. "No, they cannot join the church," the African pastor said.

I looked at him, quite puzzled, not being sure of his meaning. I asked him again in Swahili why those four people could not join the congregation with the rest who professed faith.

He smiled at me and said, "Because they are robbers and have not repented of their sins."

"Robbers?" I asked.

"Would you allow an unrepentent murderer to become a member of the church? Would you welcome an adulterer into the fellowship?"

"Of course not."

"Then I cannot admit these because they are thieves." He paused and opened his Bible. "Does it not say here," his finger pointed out the words in the text of Malachi 3:8, "Will a man rob God?" "These people have robbed God because they do not give their tithes and their offerings. As long as they continue to rob God I cannot and will not allow them to become members of this church."

2. "God needs our money," he said. "He can accomplish more good than you could possibly believe through our dollars."

The layman had taken a six-week trip to Bangladesh and other impoverished areas. He lived among the common people and came back to report to fellow Americans. He pleaded for us to help the poor and the destitute of this world.

After recounting several situations of malnutrition and starvation he had actually witnessed, he pleaded, "We must give. God needs our money to do his work!"

At least three more times during his presentation he pleaded for compassionate concern for the third world, adding, "God needs our money."

3. "We don't have a money problem," Clark said. "We have a spiritual problem."

During our board meeting we faced a problem common to many churches. The summer slump, economic depression, and people who had not kept up with their pledges. Our discussion centered on what to do about our budget, already short by 20 percent.

"Even if income picks up during December, we'll still have a shortfall of at least 15 percent," one of them said. "We've got to start cutting back now."

"Or find a way to raise more money," added a second.

Others offered their opinions.

Clark sat listening, shaking his head slowly. Finally he stood up. "We don't have a money problem. We have a spiritual problem."

Several elders stared at him, wondering what he was talking about. Clark continued, "Our problem is not that people hold back on their pledges. Not even that we're in debt and not paying our bills. We have a purely spiritual problem. We haven't properly taught our congregation, making them see the joy of sharing and their responsibility to God. They haven't seen us set the example of faithful giving either."

He started to sit down, paused, and after looking over the faces of the others, said, "Maybe when we live a life of responsible self-giving we can teach hem how it's done."

Three different approaches. Yet they represent attitudes and positions widely held within the Christian church today.

I have trouble with the position of the African pastor who would allow only tithers to affiliate with that particular congregation. He imposed a law on them, and seemed to speak very much like one of the prophets who thundered at the Jewish people. The people of Israel knew the commandments God had given to tithe (give a tenth) of their income. But simply knowing our duty does not propel most of us toward doing it. We can find reasons to excuse ourselves, even though we may feel guilty afterwards.

The man's plea to share our goods with the rest of the world was commendable. He based his plea, however, on a false premise. One thing the Bible makes clear: God does not need our money. Psalm 50:10 says that very openly. God chooses to use us, and we can be thankful that he does, but his work will be done whether through us or through some other means.

The statements by Clark represent the closest to what I believe. The whole matter of giving is a spiritual matter. We have failed to teach. Some leaders have failed to set the example. Giving also has to do with our commitment and our maturity in the Christian faith.

Let us take a quick review of giving in the Bible.

Tithing was an established custom in antiquity. We find it at least twice in the book of Genesis. In Genesis 14, Abram paid a tithe to Melchizedek. Later, Jacob, after his vision at Luz (cf. Gn 28:22), promised God that he would give a tenth of all his income. Since both these incidents occurred centuries before God gave the Law to Moses, tithing is a religious custom older than the Law, and it touches something in men.

The law of the tithe, as given to Moses, can seem rather complicated. Basically, God told them to give one tenth of all their produce, flocks, and cattle. If they lived a long distance away they could convert the goods into cash to take to the priests. Priests received the entire tithe as compensation for their service to God. The priests, in turn, gave one tenth of their income for the support of the high priest (cf. Lv 18:21-27). There also appears to have been an additional tithe, given every third year for the poor.

We learn that faithful Jews were required to give a tenth of everything, then a second tenth. Scholars disagree on whether the offering to the poor was part of the second tithe. If not, they donated 30 percent of their income! We know that, by the time of Jesus, the Pharisees had become so scrupulous about the keeping of the Law that they gave a tenth of the herbs from their garden.

Alms or almsgiving (donations to the poor) played an important role in Jewish piety. To illustrate the importance of almsgiving, it is enough to point out that the Hebrew word for it comes from the same root as the word for righteousness (*tzedakah*), and pious Jews believed that the Mosaic law gave the poor an inalienable right to certain produce of the land. This concept grew out of verses such as Deuteronomy 15:11: "There will always be some Israelites who are poor and in need, and so I command you to be generous to them." (See also passages such as Ex 23:11; Lv 23:22; Dt 24:19-22).

This law of charity toward the needy extended beyond the law of the tithe. When we come to the New Testament and the abolishment of the Law of Moses, we find no commandment on giving. Chapters 8 and 9 of 2 Corinthians speak a great deal about giving, but in a special context. Several times, in other letters, Paul refers to money collected from various churches to take to Jerusalem to feed the hungry and the poor affected by the famine referred to in Acts 11. While we find no New Testament law for tithing, giving a tenth was so ingrained in the religious life of the Middle East, we can assume that believers would expect to do so. This rings true especially when we realize that the early believers did not think they had started a new religion. Rather, they saw themselves as followers of the faith of Moses who had welcomed the prophesied Messiah.

In 2 Corinthians, while Paul does not really speak to the tithing question, he does make a very significant statement about giving in general.

> Remember that the person who plants few seeds will have a small crop; the one who plants many seeds will have a large crop. Each one should give, then, as he has decided, not with regret or out of a sense of duty; for God loves the one who gives gladly. And God is able to give you more than you need, so you will always have all you need for yourselves and more than enough for every good cause. (2 Cor 9:6-8)

The principle that Paul is enunciating is simply this: giving is a matter of faith. The farmer who plants few seeds should not expect to get much harvest. Paul also says that God is able to give us more than we need. Unless we really believe that, it is difficult for us to give in faith.

Clark spoke truly: the financial deficits were not a matter of getting more money, but a matter of faith in Jesus Christ.

I understood this a few months after my own conversion. In those days I was in the military service, living on a small monthly income. Every time the offering plate passed, I put in a dollar just like others around me did. One Sunday a Christian woman spoke at our church, telling us about how she and her husband had founded the Kerr Glass Company. For me it was a stirring testimony, built upon the principle that one tenth of their income belonged to God. She then went on to say that she believed God required 10 percent from us. If we really wanted to walk with Jesus Christ, it meant giving that tenth of our income to him.

I left the worship service troubled, especially when I considered my limited income. But I could not forget the challenge the woman had thrown at us. For several days I struggled. I kept saying, "Lord, how can I possibly give a tithe?" I figured out how much money I had coming in and my expenditures and there seemed to be no way possible. I complained several times, "God, I'm just barely making it now.

How will I handle it if I give you 10 percent?" After four days of struggling with this question, I realized that I was arguing from a lack of faith. Even though I did not know much about the Bible, I did know that if I wanted to be faithful in my commitment to Christ I had to give him at least 10 percent.

I remember coming to this conclusion and saying, "God, I don't understand how I'm going to make it if I give 10 percent of my income to you, but it's really a matter of trust. I'm holding back because I'm fearful that if I give this money to you you'll not be able to take care of me."

I read again the passage from Malachi that Mrs. Kerr had read to us that Sunday. One verse really stayed with me.

> Bring the full amount of your tithes to the Temple, so that there will be plenty of food there. Put me to the test and you will see that I will open the windows of heaven and pour out on you in abundance all kinds of good things. (Mal 3:10).

That challenged me to put God to the test. After another day of intense struggle, I said, "Okay, God, I'm willing to give you a chance. If you can still take care of me and provide for my needs if I give you 10 percent, then you're God. I'll know that you'll provide as you've promised." A sense of joy and peace came over me as I realized that I had made a commitment of my money to God—an aspect of my life that I had never given serious consideration to before.

Then it occurred to me to prove my seriousness with a real leap of faith. "Okay, God, I'll really put you to the test. I don't think I can afford to give 10 percent. But I promise that from this day on, as long as you provide for my needs, I'll never give you less than 15 percent!" That happened a quarter of a century ago. I have never gone back on my vow because God has never gone back on his provision.

The real matter of giving is not merely being aware of an obligation. It goes far beyond a commandment. When we withhold our giving we acknowledge our lack of faith in Jesus Christ. But when we give, our actions declare that God is able to provide for our needs. That is the real spiritual question involved.

Whenever I think of the whole matter of giving, the verse that comes to mind most frequently is Luke 12:34: "For your heart will always be where your riches are." If I honestly trust God's provisions for my life I do not have to be coerced into giving. I give joyfully as my response to his love. My faith says, "God has provided for my needs. Now I can be used to provide for the needs of others in response to his generosity.

We can give cheerfully to the work of Jesus Christ, and this free and joyful giving adds one more step toward a fuller self-discipline.

EIGHT

Togetherness

"AH, YOU WESTERNERS," the tall African said as he shook his head. We had been discussing his language. He was the teacher, I the pupil. I had problems with possessive pronouns. I would continually want to speak of *my* house and *my* car. Henry Nyakwana constantly corrected me, saying that I should use the word *our.*

After months of working together, I began to understand the African concept of relationship, quite different from that of the Western world. One Sunday, Henry's wife, Margaret, wore a particularly beautiful dress. The following day I saw Fibi wearing the same dress. I commented to Henry, "Your wife must have lent her the dress today."

Surprise covered his face. "No, my friend. It is the same. It belongs to my wife, it belongs to her friend. It is the same."

It took me a minute to understand what Henry meant. Their tribe did not think in categories of lending and borrowing. I began learning the marvelous concept of community from this so-called primitive tribe in East Africa. They sincerely believed in sharing what they owned. No one held the right to exclusive possession. While Henry's wife had actually purchased the dress, anyone else could use it, knowing that eventually the dress would be returned to the purchaser.

After I had worked among the tribe for more than a year I began seeing other examples. An African pastor arranged for his marriage at our local church. He did not own a coat, and asked if he could use one of mine: "Because I know you have three and I have none, may I use one?" I picked out the largest of m sportscoats. It fit him well. He wore it during the ceremon Afterward, when he and his new bride left, he still wore the coa Three weeks later, even though I had seen the newlywe several times, he never mentioned the jacket. Finally, I said him, "What happened to my coat?"

The young man looked at me in shock. "You think I a stealing it from you? Will I not return it when I have finishe with it?"

By their custom it was his to use until he had finished with i Then he would return it. That is quite a different view of li than we have. Yet in their understanding of commonality I sa our defectiveness as Westerners.

I had grown up with the concept of rugged individualism My culture and education ingrained in me that if I worked har I would succeed. I had to depend on nothing but my own skill ingenuity, and ability. I could make it alone. We constant stood in awe at the self-made tycoons, seeing them as models f us. When I came into the church I didn't have to change m concept of individualism. Most of the hymns centered o "Jesus and Me." We sang "I Will Overcome," "I Believe," an "I Am Redeemed." Preaching emphasized individual sins an personalized salvation.

I honestly believed that I did not need anybody else, as lo as I had Jesus Christ. Once I argued with a friend, "I can believe Jesus Christ holds me back from spiritual growt because of the decisions of other people. They may put u roadblocks for me, but I grow as I relate to Christ." While believed that sincerely, I also had not learned what is meant i the Apostles' Creed by the "communion of saints." We not onl need each other, but we are essential to each other's growth. has amazed me that both Old and New Testaments place heav emphasis on the fact that we belong to each other.

An extreme form occurs in the early chapters of Acts. Th first believers established a communal type of living. The encountered all kinds of problems, such as adequate serving food to widows, but they were still a community. They use words such as brother and sister, recognizing their family connections with God as their Father. We still use the terms—some groups more than others—but I wonder if we deeply recognize our family relationship to one another, and also recognize how important we are to each other.

In recent years I have learned to value the sense of belongingness in the Christian family. I find this nowhere more stimulating than in corporate worship. When I go to church on Sunday, it is like homecoming to me. I am with my family—people who love me, who understand me, and who nurture me.

Of course, Jesus Christ is with us everywhere. But we miss something vital when we separate ourselves from others. We cannot interact with a TV set. As beautiful as it may be to worship God in the beauty of nature, being with other believers makes me feel I belong. We interact with each other. When I reach out to touch God, I touch an arm made of flesh and blood.

I find the compassion of Jesus Christ when an elder says, "You look tired. Anything I can do for you?"

Jesus speaks to me when the lyric soprano hits those high notes and I sense her dedication, knowing that she has immersed herself in the music and is singing for God's people to hear.

Recently I stood at the door of our church a few minutes before the service began. Four-year-old Ben ran up, pulled me to his level, hugged me, and said, "You're my friend and I love you." He planted a wet kiss on my cheek.

In those moments when we sing together "This Is My Father's World" or "Joyful, Joyful We Adore Thee" and I hear a monotone in the third row, a decibel above the rest of us, I know I am home, among my family.

Several times in the New Testament Paul calls the church a body (cf. 1 Cor 12). Each congregation forms a body with Christ as its head. When the body functions properly, the ministries and gifts of God flow, people are nurtured, and the congregation grows in depth and in number.

What kind of life do we have when legs aren't present or an arm is missing? We have to grasp what it means to be part—and

a vital part—of a single body. It means that I have a position an
so does everyone else. Whether you sing or pray, whether
teach or usher, together we form that mystical body that mee
in that physical place. We grow together as we influence an
encourage each other. If grace comes through the proclamatio
of the Word, as I believe, then as an individual and as part of th
assembled group, we receive that grace together. And in th
receiving we bear witness to our common faith.

In my denomination we have what we call "The Directory fo
the Worship and Work of the Church." The preface reads:

> God, who chose us to be his people, calls us to serve hi
> through worship and work. Therefore the church mu
> examine its common life, and Christians their private lives, t
> the end that all may live as servants of God obeying h
> commands.
>
> Christian worship depends upon and is a response to th
> presence of God, the Father, Son, and Holy Spirit, and t
> what God has done for us and for our salvation, which w
> acknowledge by acts of adoration, confession, thanksgivin
> petition, and obedience.
>
> The church worships as believers, sharing a common li
> of faith, hope, love and commitment, assembled in commo
> public worship. Christians worship God privately as ind
> viduals and as families. We worship always as members of th
> Body of Christ.[5]

Most people will acknowledge our need to be together fo
worship. After all, Sunday worship is an American traditio
Unfortunately, though we come together week after wee
many of us never see the deeper sense of corporate worship. W
fail to take into account not only our unity in Jesus Christ bu
that each of us builds up the other. In our assembling we hav
opportunity to confess our sins, to worship God collectively, t
learn together, to be corrected together. It is a corporate act. W
are strengthened by the act of simply being together. We a
weakened by being apart from each other.

For years, I have noticed that the weakest in faith, and the most erratic in their experiences of self-discipline, are usually among the absentees of a local congregation. On the other hand, in our church choir we have a blind woman and another with multiple sclerosis. One man commented, "You don't know what it does for me when I see those two women on Sunday. They have good excuses for not coming to church. When I see them being led to the choir loft, it helps me make an effort to be here and to be part of that fellowship of courage."

The concept of our oneness has always been a part of God's plan. In the Old Testament, even though Israel consisted of twelve distinct tribes with subtribal groupings, God always viewed them as a single nation. They failed or succeeded together. Shortly after entering the promised land, the Israelites suffered defeat at a small town named Ai. When Joshua and the leaders prayed afterwards, asking God why, they heard the answer: "Israel has sinned" (Jos 7:11). As the story unfolds, only *one man* had sinned, but his sin thwarted the forward movement of the whole nation. This principle is restated throughout the Old Testament.

In the book of the Acts the concept of one body is an ongoing expression of the same theme, on a new level. So is the image of a building made without hands of which Christ is the foundation stone. Always the same principle: we belong to each other. We grow together or we hinder each other.

Self-centered, individualistic Christianity is frequently indicted. Jesus summarized the entire will of God in two great commandments (cf. Mt 22:36-40): love God with our whole being and our neighbor as ourself. In parables such as the story of the sheep and the goats in Matthew 25:31-46, one of the obvious conclusions is that God judges us by our treatment of others. We find constant exhortations, as in Galatians 6:1-3, telling us to lift others' burdens and be considerate of them. Paul writes, "As we have opportunity, let us do good to all people, especially to those who belong to the family of believers" (Gal 6:10).

We are in this together. While I do not understand all the

implications of the corporateness of the church, especially in our private, separated, exclusive living patterns, I still realize that, as John Donne said, "No man is an island."

While scarcely any Christian would dispute the clear scriptural teaching, our trouble comes when we ask, "So what? How does that affect me?" For each of us, the answer comes out differently, especially because of individual circumstances and the type of culture in which we live today.

But I can see that it means *at least* an awareness of the needs of others. Paul and his friends went from church to church collecting relief funds for the famine-stricken of Jerusalem. We follow that example when we open our hearts and minds to needs such as starvation in Bangladesh, Ghana, or anywhere else in the world.

For some, communal living may be an answer. But they have always been a minority and few have lasted long in maintaining a positive Christ-centered outlook. (The most notable exception I know of is Koinonia Farms in southern Georgia. It started in 1942 and continues today.)

For some, the concept of togetherness can begin on a level as simple as sharing beyond our immediate needs. We can open our hearts to other believers and help where we are able. It is simpler than it seems.

While our congregation in Riverdale, Georgia, presents no great model for this family centeredness, I have both seen and encouraged a trend the past few years. A group of young parents pass around baby clothes to expectant mothers. When a family moves, we have a volunteer group that assists. A mechanic spends a lot of time maintaining a car for a low-income family where the father is disabled. Our entire Sunday evening offering goes into a fund that helps many needy people.

One church I know encourages members with gardens to bring in their extra produce. Those who have no gardens then help themselves to homegrown tomatoes and corn.

One family, aware of a second family where the husband has an incurable and long-term disease, designates a portion of their offering every month to assist.

That's the family of God at work.

Small events? Yes. Insignificant? Perhaps. But these are the first steps that lead us to an awareness of the needs of others. While we need an awareness of people's needs everywhere, we start within the church family. We sensitize ourselves to brothers and sisters who have less than we do and we share.

When I read 1 John 3:17-18, I feel my failure as a Christian more than anywhere else:

> If anyone has material possessions and sees his brother in need but has no pity on him, how can the love of God be in him? Dear children, let us not love with words or tongue but with actions and in truth.

In those moments of realization, I look at myself and think of my lifestyle. Am I aware of those of my own household of faith? Am I so taken up with making it—even making it spiritually—that I overlook the struggling, the weak, the undisciplined?

This concern for community awareness becomes, for me, a distinct growing edge of my quest for spiritual self-discipline. I want to see needs as Jesus Christ sees them. I cannot help everyone but I cannot excuse myself for helping none. As I mature, I realize more fully how much I need others and how much they need me. I can expect them to care about my needs, whether spiritual or material. They fill up the lack in my life. They help where I am weak.

Self-discipline means I can't cloister myself and concentrate on *me, my,* and ignore *us* and *our.* I cannot limit this only to my own person. My self-discipline includes a concern for others. I need to reach toward them, becoming one with them, binding up their hurts, inconveniencing myself for them.

I used to visualize what would happen when I stepped into the presence of the Lord. I always hoped (perhaps influenced by schmaltzy Hollywood flicks) that I would see streaks of bright light and a white-robed figure coming toward me. Jesus would stretch out his hands to me and say, "Well done, good and faithful servant. Enter into the joy of the Lord."

A few nights ago I dreamed about entering into God's presence. A large group of us came out of a dark river (an image, no doubt, from *Pilgrim's Progress*). Others raced on ahead toward the opened gates. I saw the streams of light. I heard the angelic voices singing the "Hallelujah Chorus." I started to run, too, to join them. Then I turned and waited for two others. Only as we reached the gates of shimmering gold did I realize I held a blind child's hand and a crippled man leaned on my shoulder. When we got to the gate, it seemed to be shutting. I cried out, "Wait! We're coming."

Then I saw the white-robed figure. He was not shutting the gate at all. He was pushing his way past the crowd.

As he came closer, he smiled.

NINE

Living Sacrifices

OTHER THAN FEELING a little tired, I had no warning. Then it happened—a sudden nauseated feeling and moments later I vomited blood. The vomiting continued intermittently for two days. I ended up in the hospital. Four years later, another vomiting spell. This time I had enough sense to know what was happening. My wife rushed me to the hospital.

Both of those incidents with bleeding ulcers forced me to reflect on my life. I recall thinking, after my second hospitalization, "Will this be the pattern for the rest of my life? Every four years a trip to the hospital?" My doctor warned, "We now consider you a chronic case. You can expect to be back every three to five years."

I determined that would not be the pattern. I also prayed for my physical well-being.

While in the hospital, I began coming to grips with a theological reality: My body is God's temple and I am its caretaker. Although it took me another two years before I had worked it out in my thinking and in my behavioral patterns, I knew then what to do. I needed an exercise program!

Sounds simple. Especially these days, when people across the Western world have jumped into the physical fitness craze. But ten years ago I had difficulty convincing myself that I honestly needed exercise, that I could spend the time exercising, that it had any spiritual benefit to me. After all, my background had been among those who boasted "I never take a vacation." Our creed read, "Better to burn out than to rust out."

Over the months after my hospital release, I searched for biblical passages on exercise. I found more than I had expected. Paul uses many athletic terms and images in his letters. One reference in particular caused me to think more deeply.

In the King James Version, 1 Timothy 4:8 reads, "Bodily exercise profiteth little." I smiled, remembering one of the professors in my first year of college. He constantly encouraged students to get involved in physical activity. One day he jokingly said, "Bodily exercise profiteth little, but, thank God, it *does* profit a little." Was Paul putting down the matter of physical exercise? Or was he begrudgingly saying, "Oh, well, there is some value—not much, but some"?

A better translation reads, "Train yourself for godly living. For while physical training is of some benefit, this godly living is of benefit in every way."

To understand the apostle's intent, we have to place the incident in the context of first-century life. In Greek culture the gymnasium dominated the life of the non-slave youth of the day. In such places, young men underwent the most rigorous training to promote grace and fitness. If anything, they tended to glorify the human body. Paul is telling Timothy to realize that physical development is not enough.

The implications of the statement are simple: "You've been to the gymnasium, Timothy, and know the rigors you undergo. Discipline yourself likewise in your spiritual training." While affirming the value of spiritual exercise, Paul does not belittle the physical, but concludes that spiritual discipline bestows more. Physical rigors promote health, vitality, and beauty. Spiritual discipline promotes a fuller life that goes beyond the body itself.

Recognizing the intent of the passage gave me more of an impetus for physical exercise. That verse, along with several others, prompted me to accept *physical* exercise as a *spiritual* discipline.

Paul wrote in a day and in a culture where no one had to suggest that people needed more exercise. Our situation has absolutely reversed. We live in a culture of timesaving devices where energy-saving means saving physical energy. We no longer need to grind our flour, roll out dough, or knead bread. It is all prepackaged and done for us. We have dishwashers, instant foods, and electric golf carts. We drive to the shopping mall and if we do not find a parking spot within fifty feet of the store, we grumble and circle until a car pulls out.

The lack of demand on our physical bodies has made many of us realize that we have lost something in gaining our new world. Instead of providing the time to set aside for godliness, meditation, and worship, we find ourselves involved in a greater flurry of activities. And most of those activities put no strain on our bodies. Instead, they make us experts on headaches, stomach ailments, heart disease, and diabetes.

For centuries, Christians put a total emphasis upon personal piety, giving no consideration to the effects upon our bodies. Some of us are awakening, realizing the value of these bodies. We no longer call them "vile coverings" as a few ancient theologians did. Instead, we see them as holy temples. Paul says plainly in Corinthians that God owns our bodies (cf. 1 Cor 3:17, 6:19). *They are not our property.* By creating us and by redeeming us, God holds a double claim to our bodies.

That became my first reason for seeing physical exercise as a spiritual discipline—because caring for the physical body means caring for God's property.

I am a *unity.* God may be able to separate the physical from the spiritual, but I can't. What happens to one part of me affects my entire person.

I can only relate personal experience. Eight years ago I joined a health spa. I chose that method partially because I recognized that if I paid money for membership, I would use the facilities. I also knew that they would put me on a fitness program that I would more likely continue than if I tried exercising alone. Five years ago I began to jog. I hated the idea at first, but it began as something my wife and I could do together. We had an exciting moment when we finally reached the goal of a single mile without stopping (it took us three weeks to do that!). Eventually I increased my running and my wife went into cycling. I don't run in competitive races and do most of my running alone.

How does this affect me physically? I can list several obvious benefits. First, my health has improved. I have not been hospitalized for ulcers in eight years. My blood pressure, which had begun to creep upward to the danger level, now rests nicely at approximately 115/75. I have lost thirty pounds. Second, I feel better. I have more energy, and feel less tired out. Third, I have discovered for myself (as advocates of physical exercise have told us) that after good physical exercise my mind seems more alert and active.

Over the years I have learned other benefits of physical care. Here are a few of them.

1. It lessens stress. We all live stress-filled lives. Our modern culture with overcrowded cities, jammed expressways, high noise levels, and time-oriented activities pushes all of us. When we engage in physical activity we break out of that pattern. We shake off the stress. I find that by mid-afternoon I am wearied and my stomach is tight. For me, that is an excellent time to run. When I come back after several miles of running, I am relaxed.

2. It increases productivity. In writing or planning activities at times my mind refuses to come up with new ideas; another good time for physical exercise. Leaving the task at hand and concentrating on another activity does not mean the mind stops working. The mind now works on an unconscious level, like a stream moving underground. I have learned to expect this. Perhaps it is the need to relax the body and the muscles. Perhaps it comes from pulling away from a problem to look at a more rounded view. Whatever the reason, it works.

3. Physical benefits provide spiritual blessings. The other day Dennis and I chatted in the locker room at the spa. He is a chronic depressive type and well aware of his condition. For years he took medication. Three years ago, at his doctor's suggestion, he eased off medication and involved himself in two-hour workouts three times a week. Now, looking trim and muscular, he smiled and said, "This spa saved my life. I feel so much better about myself." His spiritual and emotional levels had a direct relationship to his physical health. "When I stop exercising even two weeks, I get depressed again. Then I just want to sit in a darkened room and I can't even pick up my Bible."

I have also learned that when my body is in top form, it is easier to overcome the spiritual battles I confront. As the metabolic process of the body speeds up, the brain, because of increased oxygen surging in, recharges itself. Creative ideas often emerge for runners when they have a "runner's high." Research indicates that the body secretes a hormone, epinephrine, that gives the athlete a sense of well-being. For me, this is all part of God's provision for the body and the spirit to work together in harmony.

Exercise does not cure everything. I am convinced, however, that physical discipline forms part of the spiritual self-discipline of God's people.

In the quarter century I have been part of Christ's church, I have never heard a sermon on the spiritual benefits of exercise (although I have preached two or three myself). In fact, I have heard little about the physical body in the church.

Yet Paul acknowledged its value in many ways. Aside from the verses already mentioned, Romans 12:1 speaks strongly. In the first chapters of the book (with a digression to talk about Israel in chapters 9-11), the apostle gives the doctrinal statements about justification by faith. Then begins the practical section, with:

> I appeal to you, therefore, brethren, by the mercies of God, to present your bodies as a living sacrifice, holy and acceptable to God, which is your spiritual worship.

He is not asking us to be martyrs or to mutilate our bodies, but to be *living sacrifices.*

Any Jewish Christian would have instantly grasped the implication of that statement. The Jews of the Old Testament knew that they could offer only animals without blemish, those which were healthy, the best of the flock. When we offer ourselves to God, what does he get? From most of us, only overstuffed, run-down, flabby-fleshed, and tired bodies. What a specimen to offer as "a living sacrifice, holy and acceptable to God."

I have had a diseased and worn-out body. I still struggle to maintain a body of which I can say to God, "I have done the best I know to take care of myself. I offer it to you as my spiritual worship."

TEN

Are You Listening?

HE HEARD THE SOFT BUZZING even before he opened his eyes. As the Reverend Paul Hanson was concluding the astoral prayer, John peeked out of slitted eyes: "Just as I hought, a fly. Is it male or female? How can you tell? How did e get in here?"

By the time the minister finished reading the scripture, John ad mentally charted the course of the fly. Mostly it circled azily around the artificial roses on Mrs. Robb's hat in front of im. Twice it landed on Mr. Bascomb's thinning hair. Being areful not to move his head, John glanced at his wife out of the orner of his eye. Nora appeared oblivious to the morning ntruder.

At 12:03, the worship service concluded. If you were to ask, ohn could tell you a lot about the fly, quite a bit about the faulty ir-conditioning, but little about the sermon.

If you are the demonstrative type, you nod at the right places, mile at the proper moments, and show studied interest in the nessage. *But do you listen?*

Over Monday coffee, Madge gives Helen an eyewitness escription of everything that took place at church the previous ay. "And, of course, Pastor Ekland gave a good sermon again."

"What did he preach about?" asked Helen.

"Oh, well, . . . I—I don't remember exactly—but it was a ood one."

We may smile at this, but it forces the question. How much *do* e listen? If you can recall one main item of last week's sermon, you score yourself a grade of barely passing (you got somethin out of the morning message). If you recall two points, you get grade of average. If you can cite the text and more than tw points, you deserve a grade of excellent: you are a good listene Take a minute to do that. How attentive are you? Attenti listening is not easy. Few people are gifted or natural listeners- most are people like you and me who have to overcome lazine and indifference. Good listening is a result of hard work an self-discipline.

One of my college professors delighted us in the classroo In the informal and free atmosphere he easily develope rapport with the students. But when he spoke (as he often di in chapel services, things were different. I found myse reviewing Greek case endings or following a fly. A delightf teacher he was; a stimulating preacher he was not! I usually le chapel empty.

Some discourses are dull, ineffective, vague. Some ministe lack directness and concreteness; some speak too rapidly; som too slowly or too softly. So we do not listen. But even in n listening we are troubled. We have been taught that when a ma expounds the Bible he is acting in the capacity of a prophet wh speaks from God to the people. He becomes the interpreter the divine will, offering us guidance, comfort, or rebuke. W assume that he has sought wisdom and eloquence in preparin his message, as well as anointing from the Holy Spirit delivering it. Then why, we ask, does he not come across?

We find ourselves perplexed and guilty. We are only to aware that the church has always taught that by the hearing the Word of God we become recipients of grace (Rom 10:17 Perhaps we are confused by that statement. What is meant that as we listen—as we understand—something happens in *u* The gospel takes on reality, becoming personal and intimat The response evoked in our hearts is "Yes, Lord, I believe When we do not find that welling up within us, we feel cheate

So I found myself after each chapel service. Knowing that th professor was a man of integrity confused me further. H prepared, I assumed, faithfully, but the message just did n nake it. Over and over I asked, what is wrong with him?

One day the realization came that perhaps I was attacking the roblem from the wrong end. Boredom was *my* problem, not is! Was it possible that I, the listener, was not hearing what God was saying through the speaker? Was it possible I was nore intent upon the buzzing of the fly than upon the roclamation of the gospel? I knew the speaker had a responsiility; grudgingly I acknowledged mine.

This self-understanding reminded me of an incident in ollege. A young student, returning a copy of *Pilgrim's Progress* e had borrowed from one of his teachers, commented, "I read t but it was dull."

With a slight grin the older man responded, "You told me omething about yourself. Now tell me something about the ook."

When we refer to a sermon, a lecture, or a discussion and add, 'I didn't get a thing out of it," we have said more about urselves than about the meeting we attended!

Unless you are unique, I suspect much of what occurs during vorship services hits you like John, who was distracted by the ly. One candid parishioner told me, "You know, for years I've repared the following week's menu during the morning vorship service." Perhaps others of us need to make similar onfessions. Our eyes turn toward the pulpit while our thoughts vatch the fly flit among the roses. We don't fall asleep or go into trance, but many of the words are tuned out. We scarcely ollow the line of reasoning.

One of the difficulties in listening we all have is in "tuning ut" a myriad of sounds. Just this morning, while listening to he radio for a weather report, I was glancing through the latest ssue of *Time.* The report was given, but I didn't hear it. The vords were spoken, the sounds came, but my attention was iveted to a magazine article. I had tuned out what I said I vanted to hear. We all have the capacity to tune out one input nd tune in another. We choose what we want to hear.

The messenger may be too thin or his suit wrinkled or his 'oice strident. But if he has a message, we must work beyond his physical attributes and listen. When I don't like the way preacher looks or acts, I remind myself of some of the biblic characters. John the Baptist wore clothes of camel skin, Elish was bald-headed, Ezekiel did strange things, and Paul seems t have had infected eyes.

Over the years, I have had to struggle to listen. Sometimes has been extremely difficult, but the rewards are worth it. Thi does not mean I always enjoy the message (for often I hav found it not to my liking, but I have understood, at any rat what the man was saying). Out of this experience I can offer yo some suggestions for more effective listening.

1. Come expecting to hear from God. This is where we ofte miss out. One summer I attended a conference with som friends. The speaker, a last-minute substitute, was a man I ha heard before. My previous experience had been uneventful; expected nothing more this time. After hearing him, my friend radiated excitement with the challenge; I, who had not give much attention, wondered what they were so excited about! got what I expected: nothing. We have to work to come with spirit of anticipation. I now make it my habit, before an sermon, to say consciously, "God is going to speak to m today."

2. Pray for the speaker and yourself. When I walk into service, I commit that time to God and ask God to spea through his servant. I try to remember to pray as he begin speaking and again during the sermon. Even while we listen, w can talk to God about the preacher and about ourselves. As w ask God to empower him, we can also pray for the message to b made clear to us individually and to the rest of the congregatio

3. Ask mental questions as you listen. When the minister make a statement not readily understood, ask, "What does he mean? He may answer later in the message. If he does not, he can b asked at the end of the service or during the week. Any faithf preacher is delighted to know people are interested enough t ask. My friend Jerry bubbled over last Monday. "I preache the Sunday evening service. For the first time since I've bee there, someone asked me about something I'd said. He didn't agree with my interpretation of the passage and we had a long talk together." Instead of feeling threatened, he was elated!

Simply because people speak from behind pulpits or lecturns doesn't guarantee they proclaim the Word of God. They may preach false messages or badly misinterpret scripture.

For example, I once heard a man talk about spiritual gifts, building his sermon around Proverbs 18:16. "A man's gift maketh room for him." He emphasized that if God gives a gift, he also provides opportunities to use that ability. Had he done more study, he would have realized that the word translated *gift* means *bribe.* The verse meant something like this: When we bribe a person, we can get what we want.

His may have been a simple error of ignorance. Sometimes people go astray from deliberate hardness of heart or by gullibly following another's false teaching.

Years ago, a gifted pastor concluded that God wanted him to live the life of a eunuch (Mt 19:12) even though he had been married for nearly twenty years. He preached a pointed sermon, telling many of the men in the congregation that if they were truly committed to Jesus Christ they would become celibate regardless of their marital status.

He was my own pastor and leader. I struggled with the admonition. I kept asking, "Is this true?" "Is God speaking to me?" I concluded that the pastor was wrong and that he had fallen into serious error.

4. Listen for yourself. A prominent minister said that in his first pastorate he decided to preach against gossip. Mrs. Lena Goodwin was the worst offender in the church, always involved in everyone's business. What she did not know, she suspected or invented and passed on as fact. He preached that morning, aiming directly at Lena Goodwin. Shaking his hand at the door, she leaned close to him, "I sure wish Mattie Jamison were here today," she whispered. "She needed to hear that sermon."

5. Think about what you have heard. Ask God to make the presented truths significant in your life.

> But be doers of the word, and not hearers only, deceiving yourselves. For if any one is a hearer of the word and not a doer, he is like a man who observes his natural face in a mirror; for he observes himself and goes away and at once forgets what he was like. (Jas 1:22-24)

6. Remember that God can speak through many channels and means. Perry had a conversion experience in a small church during the worship service. As he was leaving he told the pastor about it. The young minister, pleased at the response, inquired, "Well, just what did I say that brought about this remarkable effect?"

The new convert, looking startled, replied, "It wasn't anything you said. When we sang 'What a Friend We Have in Jesus,' I realized how much God loves me."

Good listening is the result of self-discipline and a requirement for growth. If I am serious about growing, I have to do it God's way. I cannot grow without the Bible as my foundation—and as my constant source of inspiration and knowledge.

While some understanding comes directly from the Holy Spirit to me, most of it has come through enlightened teachers who have spoken or written a truth in such a way that I grasped its meaning. And in grasping the meaning, I have grown.

As a pastor, I cannot sit in a pew each week and listen to a sermon. But I have made it a habit, for at least the past dozen years, to listen to a worship service on the radio before I go to church. I have been listening to one program at 6:30 A.M. for years. I don't like the style of preaching and often find myself disagreeing with the preacher. But even though the message may be spoken with faulty grammar, I take responsibility to sift out the chaff and hold onto the wheat. When I do, God speaks and I grow.

Listening is a spiritual discipline. Pray with the psalmist, "Open my *ears* that I may behold wondrous things out of thy law" (Ps 119:18).

ELEVEN

Giftedness

A SMILE COVERED his face and he extended a beefy arm. "Hi, I'm Bill. What's your name?"

I told him and we chatted for a brief moment about the Bible conference we were both attending.

"I have five spiritual gifts," he said. "How many do you have?"

"I—I don't know," I stuttered. "Maybe one or two."

"Just keep seeking the Lord and he'll keep adding them," Bill said, and a moment later he was gone.

That incident happened at a time when I knew little about spiritual gifts. I am not sure Bill knew much about them either. If we have spiritual abilities we do not need to point them out to other people. The gifts will speak for themselves.

I suspect that Bill was doing a little boasting. He may have been able to exercise five spiritual gifts. However, God's purpose in giving the gifts to us is to glorify Jesus Christ and not to call attention to ourselves.

Paul spoke clearly to the question of spiritual gifts.

> Now there are varieties of gifts, but the same Spirit: and there are varieties of service, but the same Lord; and there are varieties of working, but it is the same God who inspires them all in every one. To each is given the manifestation of the Spirit for the common good. (1 Cor 12:4-7)

The first lesson in spiritual gifts means we acknowledge they are just that—*gifts.* These talents are not earned possessions. They do not operate at our will but only as God allows us to use them. Most of all, God gives them to us for serving others.

It may be well to stop for a moment and define spiritual gifts. I have read current authors and talked to people who are conscious of the area of spiritual gifts. They define them differently. Some make an absolute distinction between a natural talent and a spiritual gift. Others see all abilities as spiritual gifts.

A simple way of looking at it is to acknowledge that God gives to all of us talents, so that we can serve others and bring glory to Jesus Christ. Whenever we use the abilities we have in this way, for me that constitutes exercising spiritual gifts. This may not be an accurate definition, but I think it is adequate for the purpose of this chapter.

For instance, I used to teach in the public schools. I communicate well with people. I know they respond to me. In my teaching, I can usually build a rapport between the audience and me. My ability to teach is a talent. When I take that same talent and use it to preach the Bible or in Christian education, it functions as a spiritual gift. (Of course, I could also teach English for the glory of God and in his service, but the illustration only deals with conscious intent.)

I include spiritual gifts in this book because I think this is a significant facet of the self-discipline process. As I become conscious of the gifts that God has given me it helps me to know myself and what God expects of me. It makes me aware of my usefulness to the body of Jesus Christ.

My Christian friends are all different and each exercises a different kind of gift. Pete has a marvelous ability as an administrator. He has a logical mind that automatically sets up priorities and knows the next sequential steps intuitively. Bob has what Paul calls the gift of being a helper. He does the little things that most people don't want to bother with. Instead of resenting this, he seems to delight in it. Anne has a gift for pastoring people. She teaches a Sunday school class of older adults and constantly looks after the members of her class. She always knows who is sick, who is having problems, who is rejoicing. She is always there when needed.

As I observe my friends exercising their gifts, it makes me realize that we can boldly exercise our talents. Teaching is the most important gift that God has given to me. When I go into a classroom situation I go in with confidence because I know that God has given me the ability to communicate. That does not excuse me from preparation. I must do everything I can to prepare myself, but when I am prepared and open to God, I know that I teach well.

When we use these gifts, we are assured that we are doing God's will. We all have more activities clamoring for us to do them than any of us could possibly fulfill. As I become aware of the spiritual abilities God has given me and use them, I can have a sense of fulfillment.

Of course, we never know how God might choose to stretch us or to extend our abilities. He may put us in a situation where we become aware of gifts we did not know about until the circumstance forces us to use them.[6] Sometimes we can fail to explore new possibilities for ministry. We can hold back from taking risks by saying, "That's not my gift," when we may not honestly know. If the parable of the talents means anything in terms of spiritual gifts, the principle is *"Use it or lose it."* God gives to those who use what they already have.

Marv said recently, "Most of the gifts I have developed were taken away from non-users and handed to me because I used what I had during my first forty years." Marv could be right, even though the smile on his face indicated he was kidding me.

Self-discipline and spiritual gifts come together when we explore possibilities and open ourselves to the Holy Spirit. We probably can only know our gifts by a trial-and-error method. We try one thing and then another. Eventually we will recognize a place (or places) in the body of Christ as our domain.

When I first considered the ministry, I had no idea what phase God wanted me to go into. The pastorate? Hospital chaplaincy? Military chaplaincy? College or seminary teacher?

I often questioned but had no clear guidance.

I started teaching almost by accident. Shirley and I attende a small church. I had been a Christian about a year. On morning as we walked in, the Sunday school superintenden thrust a book into my hand. "We need a teacher next Sunday fo the adult class." He hurried away, saying over his shoulder "And you're it." I gulped, took the book, and read it half dozen times during the following seven days. The book gav information but no help on how to teach the lesson. I studied prayed, complained to the Lord, and studied some more. Th following Sunday, I nervously walked into the classroom an did my best. I discovered two things. First, I enjoyed teaching Second, the people responded. A few weeks later, I became th permanent teacher for the class!

After that experience, I went to college and took numerou educational courses. I appreciate what I picked up, but th courses did not make me a teacher. I am a good teacher becaus God was pleased to give me the gift to communicate wit people.

Over the years, as I have recognized my gift, I have worked a improving it. God gave me the gift, but I have to perfect it. know I teach better today than I did fifteen years ago. As exercise my gift regularly, I become more proficient.

My friend Fran has prayed for a number of people who hav been healed. I asked her one day what she has to do to use he gift, since it seemed that all she did was lay her hands on peopl and pray for them. She responded, "It's not quite that simple. operate my gift by faith. I can't recall anyone ever being heale when I prayed for them if I didn't believe that they would be." Also, whereas she used to spend ten or fifteen minutes a da reading her Bible, she now needed at least an hour. "It's lik ammunition for me," she said. "When I have filled my hear and mind with the Bible, and I feel more in contact with th Holy Spirit, I find it much easier to pray for sick people. Whe doubts enter, I can rebuke them and not be upset or misled."

Knowing our spiritual gifts, using them, and striving t

perfect them speaks of self-discipline. We dare not take a gift for granted. No matter what the gift may be, we can always learn how to use it more effectively. God gives. We receive. Then we use these abilities in our own growth and in helping others discipline their lives so that they can become more effective for Jesus Christ.

Further, knowing and developing our spiritual gifts may look simple enough on paper. Yet, the growth process involves sensitivity to the Spirit's leading. We find ourselves faced with several choices, or roads to take, because God endows us with what seem like mutually exclusive gifts.

Without evaluating their spiritual giftedness and commitment, I'd like to point out three examples of people who had just such opportunities.

First, the late Albert Schweitzer. By age thirty he had written a monumental book in the field of musicology. In 1906 he challenged orthodox theologians with his scholarly treatise, *The Quest for the Historical Jesus.* After earning doctorates in both philosophy and theology, obtaining world renown as an organist, musicologist, and theologian, he returned to the university for a medical degree. In 1913 he went to what is now Gabon in Africa where he spent the most productive years of his life as a medical missionary. In 1952 he received the Nobel Peace Prize.

Colleen Townsend hit the top of her career when she starred in the Twentieth Century Fox production *When Willie Comes Marching Home.* Shortly afterward, she left the film industry to marry Louis Evans, Jr., a Presbyterian minister.

Dolores Hart, a leading actress in such films as the 1962 release *Lisa*, retired from public life to join a convent.

All three were prominent and talented people. They could have chosen a number of different directions. I doubt that any of them found it easy to choose. Each must have struggled with the decision. Similarly, we may have one, five, or seven spiritual gifts—any of which could lead to significant ministry. Which do we develop?

In such cases, we should remind ourselves that God gives

gifts not primarily for our fulfillment (that's the bonus!) but to glorify himself and to build up others. Part of spiritual self-discipline entails submitting ourselves to him and praying, "Lord, you tell me which direction to take."

TWELVE

Under Orders

FOR NEARLY THIRTY YEARS, George Lindsay has served as a missionary in East Africa. He has won the respect and admiration of all his co-workers, both missionaries and nationals. However, George had not planned to go to East Africa.

For years he had felt a call by God to do mission work. But he had a burden for Cuba, long before the days of the Castro regime. George had worked on the language, developed contacts with other missionaries, and was ready to assume duties on that island. Just prior to his leaving, the head of his mission board asked him if he would go to East Africa for six months. They desperately needed another worker. The present missionaries needed to go home on furlough and had no one to replace them. In six months they could send fresh recruits to the field.

Without hesitation, George obeyed. After all, he had given himself to God's service. He had also given himself to this particular mission board.

George went for six months, then six more months, then six more months. He actually stayed seven years before he came home for his first furlough.

I talked to George a few months ago. From his conversation I would never have guessed that he once had wanted to go to Latin America rather than Africa. He has served faithfully. "I know this is where God wants me," he said. George put aside his personal preference and submitted to the authority over him. He apparently had no problem submitting to the proposed change in plans. Yet, for many, the submission would not have been so simple. I can imagine any number of conversations.

> "But look at my preparation."
>
> "I've always wanted to serve God among Spanish-speaking people."
>
> "God called me to Cuba. How can you dare suggest I go o another country? Do you realize you might be interfering with God's plan for my life?"

While I do not know the conversation that actually took place, I know both George and the then-head of the mission board. Both of them are godly men who try to put God's will first in their lives. George made the change thinking it only temporary, but he obeyed willingly. He submitted to the authority over him, and went where he was needed.

In the same way, Abraham also went out, not knowing what he was getting himself into. He left his home and his family simply because God commanded.

Many of us need to learn that lesson. Whether we are talking about mission boards, volunteer activities in a local church, vocations, or neighborhood activities, we need to remind ourselves that all of us are under some kind of authority. Workers in an office recognize their supervisors. Shop foremen have authority over those under them. We recognize the responsibility of children to obey their parents and their teachers. Even our American president has those to whom he is answerable. The list goes on indefinitely. While we recognize this principle in most areas of our lives, when it comes to the gospel we want to throw off restraints.

We often get so caught up in our personal relationship with Jesus Christ and in being led by the Holy Spirit that we either ignore or fail to acknowledge those who have spiritual responsibility for us. We are not all as pliable as George. Yet yielding to authority is a firm principle of the Bible. In the New Testament, Paul exhorts people to obey the rulers over them (cf. Rom 13:1).

When the early disciples began preaching about Jesus and ealing people, the leaders of Jerusalem called them into their ouncil room. They forbade them to preach in the name of Jesus :hrist. Peter obviously recognized their authority over him as a itizen. But he recognized a higher authority when he answered, Whether it is better in the sight of God to obey man rather ıan God you judge" (Acts 4:19).

On one occasion, Peter and his fishing companions had spent ıe night in their boats and caught nothing. The next morning, esus had Peter go out in his boat again (Lk 5:4). Peter explained ıeir plight and added, "But at your word I will let down the ets" (v. 5). The story concludes with the catching of so many sh that their nets almost broke. Peter, even though he argued, nderstood and submitted to the authority of Jesus.

The nation of Israel, in starting out for the new land, had to evise a system of authority under God's leadership. Everyone ecognized Moses as a supreme authority, even though the eople sometimes rebelled. When Moses complained that the urden of hearing everybody's complaints was too much for im, his father-in-law suggested that he choose men repre-enting the tribes and family groupings to assist him. These eventy leaders handled the lesser problems and brought to him ıe more serious ones. It worked, and took much of the burden ff Moses.

On the other hand, one of the lowest points in the Old 'estament occurs in Judges. The people rebelled against God nd their leaders, only to have enemy armies come in and verpower them. They cried out, "God, deliver us." God elivered them, and after a short time they went astray again. everal times we read, "Every man did what was right in his wn eyes" (Jgs 21:25b).

Even Jesus himself, although God, spoke of his own sub-ıission as *Son* to the *Father*.

> The Son can do nothing of his own accord, but only what he sees the Father doing; for whatever he does, that the Son does likewise. (Jn 5:19)

> I can do nothing on my own authority; as I hear, I judge; an
> my judgment is just, because I seek not my own will but th
> will of him who sent me. (Jn 5:30)

> When you have lifted up the Son of man, then you will kno
> that I am he, and that I do nothing of my own authority bu
> speak thus as the Father taught me. And he who sent me
> with me; he has not left me alone, for I always do what
> pleasing to him. (Jn 8:28-29)

Paul refers to this when he says that God has put all things i
subjection under Jesus' feet.

> But when it says, "All things are put in subjection unde
> him," it is plain that he is excepted who put all things unde
> him. When all things are subjected to him, then the So
> himself will also be subjected to him who put all things unde
> him, that God may be everything to every one.
> (1 Cor 15:27-2

The principles are clear.

1. We must subject ourselves to those in authority over us. W
do this with the understanding that those over us mu
themselves answer to God. James implies that God hol
anyone in authority more strictly accountable than those i
lesser positions.

*2. If we disobey, we must recognize that we have bypassed a
authority to which we are subject.* For instance, I have alway
admired Martin Luther King because he *knew* the laws of th
land. He acknowledged that he had broken the law and wa
willing to pay for his "crime." We often break rules, not becau
we appeal to a higher authority, but because our rebelliou
nature will not obey.

*3. God requires faithfulness from us, even above service, n
matter what our position in God's kingdom* (1 Cor 4:3). Part o
faithfulness entails obeying those who have authority over u

When we make decisions, we pray for God's guidance. When answers come to us, we must check them out by submitting them to those over us.

For example, in our denomination we have what we call an Executive Presbyter, a leader with somewhat less authority than a bishop has in other denominations. Some years ago, I felt it was time to leave my first parish and had already begun to talk to a pulpit committee from another state. This is the normal procedure, but because I believe in being submissive to authority, I contacted our Executive Presbyter and told him of my plans. He answered, "I like the work you've done and would hate to lose you from this area. Would you give us a chance to find another pastoral situation for you before you make any final decisions about where you're going?"

Within two months I was in a new pastoral situation in the same geographic area. As I look back now, I see God's guidance in this. I did not know about the particular church needing a pastor. I know only that I yielded myself to the authority over me. My superior in the divine chain of command then turned the wheels.

At a later time, I decided to leave the pastoral ministry altogether. After much prayer I contacted the Executive Presbyter. In essence, he said, "Don't do it. You're tired. Wait four months and see if you feel the same way." By taking his advice, I did not leave. I almost made a serious mistake, but by bowing to the person in authority over me, I averted it.

As a pastor, when I want to make a significant decision that affects my ministry or the congregation, I have an official board of elders which we call the Session. I learned long ago to trust this board. They are elected as representatives from our congregation. I submit ideas and plans to them. After they have heard me, they offer their perspective and sometimes vote to support me. At other times, they have said no. In almost all those instances I have been able to accept it graciously simply because I believe they are the authority over our local congregation.

Naturally, authorities can be wrong. During the Hitler era in

Germany, as the demands and restrictions grew, many churc leaders yielded. They felt they were obeying the authority ove them. Others, such as Martin Niemoeller and Dietric Bonhoeffer, resisted. These resisters, believing their cause jus were willing to pay the consequences for their disobedience.

Acknowledging authority recognizes that none of us is a isolated individual. We each form parts of the whole and ar members of a single body. In our seeking to do God's will, w must recognize that God himself has put us in submission t others, to help us see our own sinfulness and tendency towar waywardness. Appealing to someone over us enables us to hav a check-and-balance system in our lives.

I remember a famous evangelist of the 1950s. I had questior about healing until I met that man and saw him in action. O one occasion, I attended a five-day conference and he preache every night. When he prayed for the sick, I saw many peopl healed, night after night. At the same time, his preachin disturbed me. He had little theological knowledge and often fe into gross error. For instance, he became convinced that the si in the garden of Eden was that Eve had intercourse with th serpent. That influenced every doctrine he believed and taugh He shut himself away from other ministers and teacher refusing to listen. To my knowledge, to the day of his death, h refused to acknowledge any human authority over him.

On the other hand, I have a friend who helped start charismatic prayer group in his local church. For a number c months things went smoothly, the group increased, and man people could look back upon the experience as healthy an helpful. After two years, the pastor called my friend and tw other members of the group aside. He felt that they wer becoming lopsided and were in error in some of the things the were doing. He asked my friend to remove himself from th position of authority and, for a period of at least six months, t allow someone else to lead. Consequently, my friend told th members of the group that, in obedience, he was taking n leadership role.

During the first weeks after he abdicated leadership, m

friend battled within himself. He struggled with resentment, anger, bitterness, rejection, and he questioned whether he ought to leave that local congregation and go elsewhere. He read his Bible and prayed more than ever before. It became a real test of submission to authority. After several weeks of intense prayer, he surrendered. He continued attending the prayer group, week after week. At first he sat in the back with minimal participation. As the days wore on, he took more of an active role. At the end of six months, the pastor said to him, "You're ready to lead again."

"And you were right in asking me to step down," my friend said.

Later, one of the group said to him, "You taught us a great lesson by obeying the pastor. If you had left the church, at least forty of us would have been right behind you."

As I have sought to center my life in Jesus Christ, I recognize that part of that centering comes from submitting myself to the authority over me. When I do that I merely follow orders—divine orders.

For me, as one Christian, yielding to authority works this way. When I search for God's direction, I know that I can be deceived by my own self-centered needs, that I have blind spots and prejudices, and that I sometimes focus on a problem so long I lose sight of the larger picture. God has put checks and balances in the body of Christ into his scheme for my life. My actions can never be totally my own choice, independent of anyone else. No matter what my position, I will always have someone over me. God intended it that way. My self-discipline involves submitting joyfully to those over me, especially when they direct me in a path different than one I wish to take.

When you are tempted to go it alone think of Jesus himself.

> During the days of Jesus' life on earth, he offered up prayers and petitions with loud cries and tears to one who could save him from death, and he was heard because of his reverent submission. (Heb 5:7)

Notice that he was heard because of his *reverent submission.*

I want to be heard in my prayers because of my reverent submission.

THIRTEEN

Share the Faith

JERRY AND I TRAVELED from the United States to East Africa with a stopover in Europe. I noticed that whenever we got on a plane, within five minutes Jerry had already started talking comfortably with someone seated near him. Another three minutes and he had explained we were making our trip to revisit places in Africa where I had once been a missionary. From there he led the conversation into talking about Jesus Christ. Time after time I marveled at the skill with which he moved the conversation in a spiritual direction. I, on the other hand, find it harder to talk to strangers about anything. He is not the better Christian because words flow more easily with strangers. Jerry and I are just two different kinds of people.

While Jesus exhorted his disciples to proclaim the gospel to every creature, he did not call us all as evangelists. Some people have the ability to recruit for the kingdom. They do it with such ease that people do not feel they are being forced or pushed into anything. Not all of us have that ability. Even though we cannot all call ourselves evangelists, however, we are not free from the great commission to evangelize. We must do our evangelizing differently.

Over the years, I have tried to do the work of an evangelist repeatedly, and failed every time. But I do have a concern for people. I want to see others brought to Jesus Christ. Since I don't find it easy to confront people with their need for God, my style is to take a different approach.

Last Sunday, for instance, I walked into the church hall

where we serve a continental-type breakfast. Most of the people congregated in groups of three or four, talking quietly with friends. I also saw two new people standing by themselves. I hurried to the first one, introduced myself, and chatted briefly. Then I introduced him to someone else close by. "This is Gary. He's new. How about introducing him around?" Then I introduced myself to the other stranger.

Some would call this simply being gracious to strangers. Few would call it direct evangelism. Yet I call it evangelism, recruitment, even outreach. I want newcomers to feel wanted and accepted. If they perceive us as a group of caring people, they may then open themselves to God. I always hope they will eventually make the transition to realizing that God enables us to care.

Most people will never be evangelists in the strict sense of the word. Yet we can open ourselves to include others in our worlds. It always saddens me that during free time at church activities, most people talk only to their friends. Few search out the loners and strangers. Searching out new faces would mean not so much *telling* the good news as *living* the good news. If our living actually is a viable form of evangelism, we need to pray about the way we treat others and reflect upon those actions afterward. Sometimes our living contradicts our telling.

A few years ago, a man visited our church for the first time. He came early and I had an opportunity to talk to him for two or three minutes. I found out where he worked and said, "We have someone in our congregation who also works there." I mentioned the member's name.

"Oh, this is where he goes to church?" he said. He was not smiling.

"Do you know Don?"

"Yes, I know him," the stranger answered. "He's a supervisor in the department next to mine. He's not very well liked, you know."

"No, I didn't know that," I said, not sure what to say.

"Oh, he talks about God regularly but he's also a man who

loses his temper and has more people transferring out of his department than anywhere else."

Someone interrupted us, and I didn't have an opportunity to say anything more. The man slipped out of church before I had a chance to speak to him again. He never came back. I wondered many times if Don's example at work prevented this man from coming back to worship with us again.

On the other hand, a young couple from our church went through a severe crisis when their two-year-old daughter became suddenly ill. They rushed her to the hospital where she remained in a coma for two days and died. Nearly a year later, a nurse from that hospital came to our church. "I've been wanting to come for a long time," she said, "but I'm a shy person. I finally got up the courage." She told me a little about herself and then said, "Bob and Velma really drew me to this church. I worked the night shift much of the time when their child died. I saw the way they went through that agonizing time. While they were full of pain, especially after they knew the child would probably not live, they still had such a calmness about them, even when they cried. I knew they had something that I didn't have."

This leads me to believe that one of the significant marks of discipline in a modern Christian's life is that we become careful about the way we live our Christian faith. As we read through the New Testament, we see that Paul wrote great doctrinal statements to the church in the first half of almost every letter. The second half was devoted to the practical living of the gospel of Jesus Christ. While we know that God holds everyone responsible for himself or herself, we also know that the way we live influences others.

My handwriting has a natural backward slant to it. I had never thought very much about it until after I started teaching sixth grade. About the third week of school, I realized that almost every child was turning in papers imitating my back-hand. Was this the way I wanted these children to write? I wanted them to write as nearly as possible the way the penmanship book had outlined for them in the fourth grade. In order for them to write that way, I had to make some changes in *my* penmanship. I went to the fourth grade teacher and asked her for the penmenship book. For the next two weeks I worked hard at making my handwriting resemble as closely as possible the method taught in the school. Not long after that, I noticed that the children imitated my better form of penmanship.

It doesn't matter what we do, whether it is the way we write or talk or behave, we all influence people. Self-discipline involves taking responsibility for that influence.

A few years ago, the men in our church played in a basketbal league. We were the outsiders; all the other teams belonged to another denomination. They also furnished the referees. Each week our men complained about the unfair tactics of the othe teams and of the referees' obvious prejudice against us. Halfway through the league season, Charlie dropped off the team. " kept losing my temper," he said. "I didn't think I provided very good example of Christian love standing out there yelling at obvious inequities." Charlie couldn't answer for his team mates or for the league, but he could answer for himself. " wasn't demonstrating the goodness of God on that court."

Charlie perceived the situation well. Most of us are no always that perceptive. Watch people waiting in long lines at th grocery store. Watch them driving in heavy traffic, especiall when someone cuts in ahead of them. That is when thei influence—negative or positive—really comes out.

Our evangelism centers around the way we live. We share o deny the faith each day of our lives. How we act in unguarde moments tells the real story about us. Jesus said, "By their fruit you shall know them" (Mt 7:16).

In East Africa, there was a school teacher named Abdu Yusef. A staunch Moslem, he was the best-educated Indian i that community. I frequently saw him in the small shops wher we bought our provisions. One day he started chatting with m and said, "I don't know much about your God but I think if could see him he would look something like you."

I was so amazed that I didn't know how to respond. I mus

have simply stared at him. He said, "I think you must serve a very happy God because he makes you happy. You are always smiling." He and others in that part of Africa began calling the Christians that I worked with the "hallelujah people" out of respect. They said, "You always praise God and are happy in your religion." Eventually, he confessed to me his faith in Jesus Christ. He often said it was seeing the happiness of Christians that first interested him.

To spread a positive influence means keeping a guard on our own selves. It does not mean being hypocritical. It means doing more than rattling our mouths about Jesus Christ. Sometimes constantly talking about God may even produce a negative influence. I know of one denominational headquarters which hired several new employees zealous for Christ. They got so busy running around the building talking about Jesus that they neglected their work. The other Christians in the building were as committed as the talkative ones, but they realized that, at work, their jobs came first. In the long run, the second group had the more positive influence.

To discipline ourselves, we begin to think about our words and actions beforehand and reflect on the words we have said and the actions we have done. If we can become masters over our words and actions we become not only more disciplined but also better witnesses to Jesus Christ.

FOURTEEN

Endure

I NEVER SHOOK my fist at God. I never shouted obscenities at him. But I often questioned him, and several times my anger blazed. "God, why are you treating me this way?" I yelped. Doubts of his love filled my head. Those questionings and doubts had to be expressed because they came from my heart.

During the early years of my Christian experience, God often seemed to let me down. Life would zoom along smoothly, filled with spiritual progress and visible results, then, kerplunk, everything (or so it seemed) went wrong. Then I would erupt again, feeling a whole range of emotions—anger, frustration, guilt, self-recriminations, doubts. Phases came and went. Bad experiences followed on the heels of good. Somehow, each time, I pulled out of the pit and life went well for another few weeks.

I often prayed that I could live a consistent life and not let problems overwhelm me. I would experience a period of peace and the presence of God. Then, often without warning, another low blow in life would shake me. "I'm your child," I reminded God. "Why are you doing this to me?"

I wonder how I would have responded if God had answered: "Son, you're growing. You need to overcome this obstacle to prepare you for greater challenges in life." Probably I wouldn't have understood.

Besides, I didn't care about knowing that I would grow stronger in the future; I hurt in the present. When I said to my then five-year-old daughter, "This spanking is going to hurt me more than it does you," she said, "I'm the one who cries."

I grounded my third-grade son when he played in the street. "I want you to learn from this," I told him.

"You always say that, Daddy," he replied. "Anytime you punish me, it's supposed to teach me something. I'm tired of learning things."

I have often prayed, "God, I'm tired of learning painful lessons. Just *tell* me so I don't have to learn by enduring so much pain." Unfortunately, we learn little from just hearing instructions. We learn most of our important lessons from experience. We can learn from our successes in life, but we learn from our failures, too. The Bible says of Jesus, "But even though he was God's Son, he learned through his sufferings to be obedient" (Heb 5:8). Obedience is *learned,* and primarily through the experience of suffering.

"Negative reinforcement" is a learning device. We know that if we touch fire, we get burned. If we overload our food with salt, it tastes briny. Most of us caught on early that disobeying parental instructions ensured us of some kind of punishment.

But some suffering comes to us for doing right.

In Acts, soldiers dragged the apostles before the Jewish leaders, who rebuked, threatened, beat, and even imprisoned them for preaching Jesus Christ. Paul and his entourage often suffered persecution. Stephen and James were martyred.

Our doing right may not be as dangerous as going to strange lands and preaching the message of Jesus Christ among hostile people. Our suffering may come from simple things like speaking against racial prejudice, refusing to participate in activities that offend our consciences, or advocating unpopular views because we believe in them.

I remember that, a few months after my conversion, our department cooperated in a Navy Relief fund-raising drive. I had no problem with helping people less fortunate. Our department, however, chose to handle all the gambling booths.

For two days I struggled with the issue. As a Christian, my conscience would not allow me to encourage gambling, even for a worthy cause, since it espoused the idea, subliminally, that we can get something for nothing. I went to my superior officer and xplained that I simply could not feel right about participating. Of course, if you order me, then I'll do it," I added. He, eeming to understand my position, exempted me from the uty. But two others in the department made jeering remarks fter they found out.

"Hey, Preach, you ought to go over there and turn over those ambling tables," one said. "Chase everyone out with a big hip."

"Why don't you go over and taste a little of that sin," the ther mocked. "Sin's real fun. You might even learn to enjoy ."

Though my sense of integrity meant more than their jibes, I ill smarted from the remarks.

I learned later that God exempts no one from hardships, isunderstandings, jeers, and rebukes (2 Tm 2:3). Whenever e make our commitment to Jesus Christ, the evil forces of this orld will try to thwart us. Our commitment will undergo ountless tests.

Many who in the 1960s took the unpopular stand in favor of vil rights, endured abuse, hatred, suspicion, even actual ersecution. Their friends misunderstood them and turned gainst them, but they stood their ground.

Long after the strains of "We Shall Overcome" died out, a vil-rights demonstrator said, "I never want to go through that gain, but I wouldn't want to have lived without going through once." He went on to tell me how much he had learned during at period. I expected him to talk about bigotry, inhumanity, id rejection.

Instead, he said things such as, "I learned to love people who ere different from me. I learned what it meant to share, when ou had nothing to eat but a loaf of bread and a half a jar of ayonnaise among ten people in one room. I learned what it as like to sleep on a cold floor and to be thankful just for a place lie down." He went on to tell me that he had joined in the vil-rights movement because he was an idealist and was nvinced that they stood for just principles. "I didn't really iderstand what was happening, or how deeply ingrained our prejudices are," he said, "but I soon learned."

When we met, I immediately thought of him as a man of dee compassion. He identified with the poor and the needy. He ha adopted a simple way of life and needed few of the things th most of us call essentials.

Most of us will not go through hardships that involve suc privation or fear for our lives. But if we determine to live disciplined and faithful life, we will have our share.

I just got off the telephone. A woman who had once been a active member of our congregation poured out her tale marital infidelity, and the guilt that gave her no peace. I spoke t her of Christ's forgiving love. After nearly an hour, she thanke me for listening and said, "You're so open and easy to talk to. After she hung up, I smiled to myself. I have not always bee open. I was once as closed and intolerant of failure as anyon could be; my rigid set of beliefs and values allowed for no gra areas in life. I have come a long way, and I am convinced that owe much of my openness to hard experiences the Lord took m through.

During my years as a missionary in Africa, I realized ho volatile I was, how often anger controlled my actions. M tongue often got me into trouble. Sometimes I simply spoke to frankly. At other times my words were right but my attitud wrong. Sometimes I loved too little, spoke too loudly, an criticized too harshly.

I had taught the Africans, "If you have any problems, yo only have to ask Jesus Christ and he'll help you take care them." Many nights I wept and cried out to God to help m control my words. Then, a few days later, I would find myse sternly rebuking people who disagreed with me. Once a African brother said, "Haven't you prayed about your ange Surely, God will help if you do." My own words coming back me increased my misery.

My first three years in Africa were painful, but they force me to examine myself. My experiences made me realize that li is not always simple and neat. I did pray, and God did answe but between the prayer and the answer I had lessons to learn.

One was that I am basically a sinful person. That is hard to acknowledge. I have always liked believing that I am a good person who operates from basically good motives. Facing up to my careless words and angry actions forced me to realize that I had failed God in many, many ways. I had not had compassion when it was needed. I had not understood simple explanations because my heart was hard.

I have had to go through many difficult times. I cried out to God for help. I also wondered why he allowed my life to be so difficult. Yet I can nearly always look back and say I learned from that experience. Not until the mid-1970s did I really understand death. I had been in the ministry for several years and had often offered comfort to the bereaved. Then, in a period of two years, both my parents died, an older brother, a nephew, a brother-in-law, and two very close friends.[7] I knew then what it was to lose loved ones, firsthand. I went through the stages of grief that I had observed in other people. Previously, I had known about grief in my head; now I knew it in my heart.

What have suffering and hardship to do with self-discipline? We learn through hardships many lessons we could grasp no other way. Recently, in a Bible study, Woody said, "It seems that every time I go through a hard place and feel ready to give up, I manage to make it through. Then, almost without fail, a week later I'll read a book or hear a sermon about what I've just learned. I keep thinking, I wish I'd had that book before I went through the hard time."

"But would you have honestly learned anything?" a member of the group asked. "Reading would have exposed a good spiritual principle, but it wouldn't have meant much to you until you actually went through it yourself."

Another reason for the hard times in our lives is chastisement. In the Bible, *chastisement* (discipline) always refers to God's people, while *wrath* refers to the wicked. Chastisement happens for our good, to turn us around. Wrath falls upon those already so hardened that they refuse to listen to God's love.

> "For the Lord disciplines him whom he loves, and chastise every son whom he receives." It is for discipline that yo have to endure. God is treating you as sons; for what son i there whom his father does not discipline? If you are le without discipline, in which all have participated, then yo are illegitimate children and not sons. (Heb 12:6b-8)

Going through hardships and suffering can actually bring abou joy in our lives, if we know that we are passing from spiritu infancy into maturity.

A man came to my office one day and told me how he ha built up a great business, grossing over $100,000 a yea Through a series of events over which he had no control, th business fell and he ended up bankrupt. As I started to expres sympathy, he smiled and said, "And now I'm free. I can sta over again and this time, I promise to put God first. I'm happie than I've been in a long time. I keep thanking God for makin me fail so that I could understand what really is important i life." That man had moved from being a babe toward becomin a mature son.

The New Testament distinguishes between spiritual babe and sons (cf. Heb 5:11-14). *Child* or *babe* refers to the spirituall immature who have not progressed in their commitment. Whe a boy reached the age of majority in ancient Rome, peop regarded him as an adult. Sons, as in Romans 8:14 ("For all wh are led by the Spirit of God are sons of God"), show wisdo and understanding of spiritual truth. A child doubts, a son sure. A child balks, a son obeys. A child wonders, a son know

I started by saying that I have often questioned God. I hav sometimes been angry at the way life has gone for me. I hav needed answers, assurance. I now find, however, that I ask "Why, God?" less often. This indicates progress in my spiritu development. I don't like hardship, and I still resist disciplin but I also know that God allows only the sufferings necessa for my next step of commitment and self-discipline. For year when things went wrong in life I felt like a child in the dark. I reached out for my Father's hand and asked, "Are you really with me, Lord?" Now when I walk through darkness I have the assurance that he is there whether I feel his presence or not.

I have learned the message of Hebrews 12:2. "Keep your eyes on Jesus, our leader and instructor. He was willing to die a shameful death on the cross because of the joy he knew would be his afterwards." Jesus could endure hardship because of what awaited him. Part of the growing thrust of my life involves facing the hard moments. Though I am now learning that afterwards I will be stronger and closer to Jesus Christ, I still often fall back on the words Paul wrote to young Timothy in his moments of wavering: "Take your share of suffering as a good soldier of Christ Jesus" (2 Tm 2:3).

FIFTEEN

Discipling

ALTHOUGH I HAVE NOT seen Barry Grahl in more than twenty years, I will always have a special place in my heart for him. He was my first teacher in the Christian faith. Today I would probably say that he discipled me.

I had come to Jesus Christ after an intense struggle to understand myself, my world, and the Bible. Shortly afterward, Barry transferred to our naval base. He was a lanky fellow whose constant smile radiated his commitment to Jesus Christ. In the year we served together, Barry taught me a great deal. He involved me in systematically reading the Bible and especially in memorizing. About the time we went different ways, an older Christian named Chuck came into my life and spent hours every week with me. Chuck said to me, "I sense a hunger in your life, and I think God wants me to help you."

These men treated me as Paul treated Timothy and Titus. He saw them as his spiritual offspring. His letters to them (often called the Pastoral Epistles) reveal the action of a caring Christian for the progress of two younger men in their spiritual pilgrimage.

As I have thought of the Christian life and the self-discipline of believers, this aspect of true discipleship must come into focus somewhere. If we are to move ahead spiritually, we need a model—a human being who challenges us by example and by words. We all need someone to disciple us. We usually have one (or even more) such person even though we may not always recognize him or her. We may call that person our teacher, spiritual confessor, leader, or simply friend. That individual is someone farther along the spiritual road. That person does not turn back, but pauses long enough to grab our hand and pull us onward. Every *growing* believer stretches out a hand toward someone. (Of course, one can be both a disciple and a discipler, still learning while reaching out and teaching others.)

We have ample biblical illustrations of the disciple and the discipler. Moses took Joshua, trained him, and kept him by his side. When Moses died, the disciple Joshua took charge. Hundreds of years later, the great prophet Elijah took Elisha as his disciple. Even the apostle Paul did not start out as a spiritual giant. Acts 13 and 14 tell us that Barnabas took him by the hand, sponsored him, and brought him into prominence in the church. Later, Paul apparently outgrew his teacher, went on his own, and developed his own disciples. But for the first stages, Paul had someone holding his hand.

I emphasize discipleship because I believe that no Christian grows in isolation from other Christians. God plans that we grow in community with one another. My knowledge does little good unless I am willing to share it with you. Your experiences and growth enrich me as you tell me what you have learned. Most families operate this way. My oldest child became the example and the teacher for the two younger ones. In God's family, it is the same.

"How fortunate," someone said, "that Jesus called them disciples rather than wise men. Disciples don't stop growing." In the ancient world, a teacher with a small band of followers operated in the way schools and universities operate today. Discipleship means learning. We place ourselves under the tutelage of the Holy Spirit, who works through people to instruct us.

We start as disciples much as we did in school. If we follow instructions, we progress. One day we are able to say to someone else, "I've traveled a short distance up the road and know what it's like up ahead. Let me take your hand and we'll make the journey together."

Becoming the discipler is not a matter of pride or of spiritual arrival. It simply means that one person is a few steps ahead of the other. When one person disciples another, the process has in mind a single focus: spiritual maturity. Both grow through the experience. Discipling forces the discipler into self-examination, re-thinking attitudes, and clearer theological thinking. "If I'm asking someone to follow my pattern," a friend said, "I don't want to give him a crooked pattern to follow."

How do we go about the process of discipleship? Consider these ideas.

1. Find out where you are. What is your own assessment of your spiritual level? The question is not "How long have I been in the church?" or "When was I confirmed?" Are you a spiritual babe, able only to drink milk (cf. 1 Pt 2:2)? Are you far enough along the road to say, "I'm ready to help someone else. I've been taught and now it's my turn"?

2. Seek a model. Paul boldly told the Ephesians to imitate him. We need human models who point us to Jesus Christ. As I reflect on both Barry and Chuck, I can see their imperfections as human beings. Yet they both evidenced qualities that drew me to them and, ultimately, toward Jesus Christ.

3. Be willing to learn. I often had to pray, "Make me teachable, Lord," when I sat at the feet of others.

For the past few weeks I have been listening to the radio as I drive between hospitals and appointments, a gospel station that broadcasts a different preacher every half hour. The style of preaching is not to my taste and, at first, I didn't expect to learn a lot from those preachers. But I soon realized that, despite their lack of education, God does use them. (A portion of me insists on adding, "And God would use them even more if they polished up their English a bit.") Some days I find it harder to listen than others, but I don't want to miss anything just because of my prejudice. The Jewish leaders, noting Peter and John as ignorant men (cf. Acts 4:13), did not listen. I don't want to be locked into that category. As long as God is pleased to give me life, I want to keep growing.

4. Be willing to outgrow. Sir Isaac Newton said something lik this: "If I have seen further than others it is because I hav stood on the shoulders of giants."

In time, a pupil may outshine the teacher. Elisha asked hi mentor for a double portion of the Spirit. We have eigh recorded miracles done by Elijah, and twice that many b Elisha. The ministry of Elisha seems more far-reaching tha that of his predecessor, but I doubt that Elijah would hav minded. If you are the discipler, train those who follow t outgrow you. That is the greatest service you can do for them o for yourself.

In 1971, I began to write because Charlie Shedd encourage me. Since then, I have taught others the principles of writing Two of my writing disciples have ability that exceeds mine. honestly rejoice in their growth. Most of all, I am excited t know that we walked together until they outran me.

The heart of Christian discipleship is the process of bein taught by someone while trying to help others move forward.

"But," you might ask, "is every Christian capable of actuall discipling other Christians?"

Of course not.

That doesn't mean we sit back and say, "I'm not able." suspect that many people who helped me along the way didn' even recognize the effect they had on me. But beyond that, if w honestly grow in our own faith, the natural tendency is to pass i on. Perhaps it will help to look at the matter this way: I am th father of three children. I have tried to teach them abou life—everything from how to live and set their priorities, t learning to establish their own values. I have done it not onl because God holds me responsible to be a good parent bu because I love my children. I want the best for them. I yearn fo their growth.

As I see others in God's family struggling, I want to offe them my hand, to guide them into greater maturity. At the sam time I'm pressing ahead as I follow my own spiritual mentors

Some Christians don't grow much themselves, so they hav little to offer. Discipling implies a certain amount of spiritu development. Further, discipling may not entail formal instruction or guidance. It may simply require that you become a role model and put into actions what you may not be able to put into words.

I hope all Christians want to grow enough so that they can disciple others. Paul had to rebuke Timothy several times in the two letters he wrote (implying that Timothy was young and needed to shun youthful sins, that he was lazy and needed stirring up, that he had poor health and needed medical advice about wine for his stomach). Even so, he said, "Timothy, the things I have taught you now become your responsibility to instruct others who are faithful so that they, too, might disciple others" (see 2 Tm 2:2).

SIXTEEN

One Thing More You Lack

THE STORY OF the rich young man who approached Jesus comes to mind. He knew all the commandments and, according to his own testimony, kept them. So far as he knew himself, he probably did. Jesus certainly never made any accusation against him, nor did he argue the point of the young man's obedience. He simply said, "You still lack one more thing." Jesus told the man to sell everything he had and turn the money over to the poor. "But when he had heard these things, he became very sad; for he was extremely rich" (Lk 18:23). Jesus had touched his vulnerable spot and the man turned back.

In the light of that story, I am afraid to end a book like this with the idea that if you practice self-discipline in these areas, you will have mastered everything in the Christian life. In fact, God will always reveal new areas to each of us, and these areas will vary from person to person.

I know where the Holy Spirit wants me to exert my next effort of self-discipline: *the words I speak.* I am growing increasingly aware of my need to edit my speech, just as I edit the material I write.

It is easy for me to say too much or to tell only a partial truth by holding back information or to mislead by silence. I justify my actions and defend myself against even implied accusations. I sometimes defensively put myself down so that others won't get the chance! I belittle others out of jealousy. Sometimes I speak too quickly, ready to give an answer before I have even heard the question.

Need I go on? This is a little of my current spiritual battle. I have not won—*yet*—but I am not discouraged either, at least most of the time. Even when I am, I take courage in the fact that at least I realize my mistakes and failures. I didn't always. On the other hand, I do have moments of great victory and clarity. I simply do not have enough of them.

When a couple returned from vacation, they were telling me about the awful time they had in going through customs in Egypt. I found myself anxiously waiting for them to pause so I could tell them about the time we went through customs in Jordan. My account was so much more exciting than theirs. I had to ask myself, "Exciting to whom?" To me, of course. Yet to interject my experience would have been to diminish theirs, even though they might not have interpreted it that way. While trying to listen to all the details, the argument went on in my head. I kept my mouth shut and silently thanked God for helping me be quiet.

This is my current area of struggle for spiritual mastery. Eventually I am going to win, too, because I am on the side of the greatest Winner of all!

So are you. Whatever "one more thing you lack" in self-discipline, God will show you and lead you to victory in it. Be diligent in seeking the fullness of his life and grace.

Notes

rother Lawrence, *The Practice of the Presence of God* (Old Tappan, New rsey: Fleming H. Revell Co.), p. 17.

am aware that religious leaders of the day taught a formula prayer to their mediate followers. The disciples asked Jesus for a prayer like John had ught his devotees. Yet I believe they asked for more than specific words to peat.

ristian bookstores carry several different Bible memory programs. My vorite is the modified Topical Memory System, put out in a kit by Navigator ess. It includes everything needed to memorize sixty verses.

e question of hunger arises while fasting. Some people say they never feel ngry. Others tell me that they battle it constantly for at least the first three ys. I have had both experiences.

esbyterian Church in the United States, *Book of Church Order* (Atlanta: nn Knox Press, 1980).

ave written more about spiritual gifts in my book *Getting There from Here* 'aco, Texas: Word Books, 1981).

ter the death of my brother, father, and two friends, but before the loss of nephew and brother-in-law, I wrote *Comforting Those Who Grieve* tlanta: John Knox Press, 1979) to express my own pain as well as the nfort I experienced through others.